ANGELS®

ES

INSIGHT EDITIONS

P.O. Box 3088, San Rafael, CA 94912

www.insighteditions.com

Library of Congress Cataloging-in-Publication Data available.

ISBN: 978-1-60887-019-6

🌲 REPLANTED PAPER

Insight Editions, in association with Roots of
Peace, will plant two trees for each tree used in the
ROOTS of PEACE   manufacturing of this book. Roots of Peace is an
internationally renowned humanitarian organization dedicated to
eradicating land mines worldwide and converting war-torn lands
into productive farms and wildlife habitats. Together, we will plant
two million fruit and nut trees in Afghanistan and provide farmers
there with the skills and support necessary for sustainable land use.

Manufactured in China by Insight Editions

10 9 8 7 6 5 4 3 2 1

UNDER THE HALO

THE OFFICIAL HISTORY OF ANGELS BASEBALL

WRITTEN BY
PETE DONOVAN

FOREWORD BY
TIM SALMON

PREFACE BY
ARTE MORENO

INTRODUCTION BY
MIKE SCIOSCIA

INSIGHT EDITIONS
San Rafael, CA

GENUINE C243 Rod Carew LOUISVILLE SLUGGER

GENUINE C243 Ryman Babock LOUISVILLE SLUGGER

GENUINE R161 LOUISVILLE SLUGGER

Powerized

Powerized

Powerized

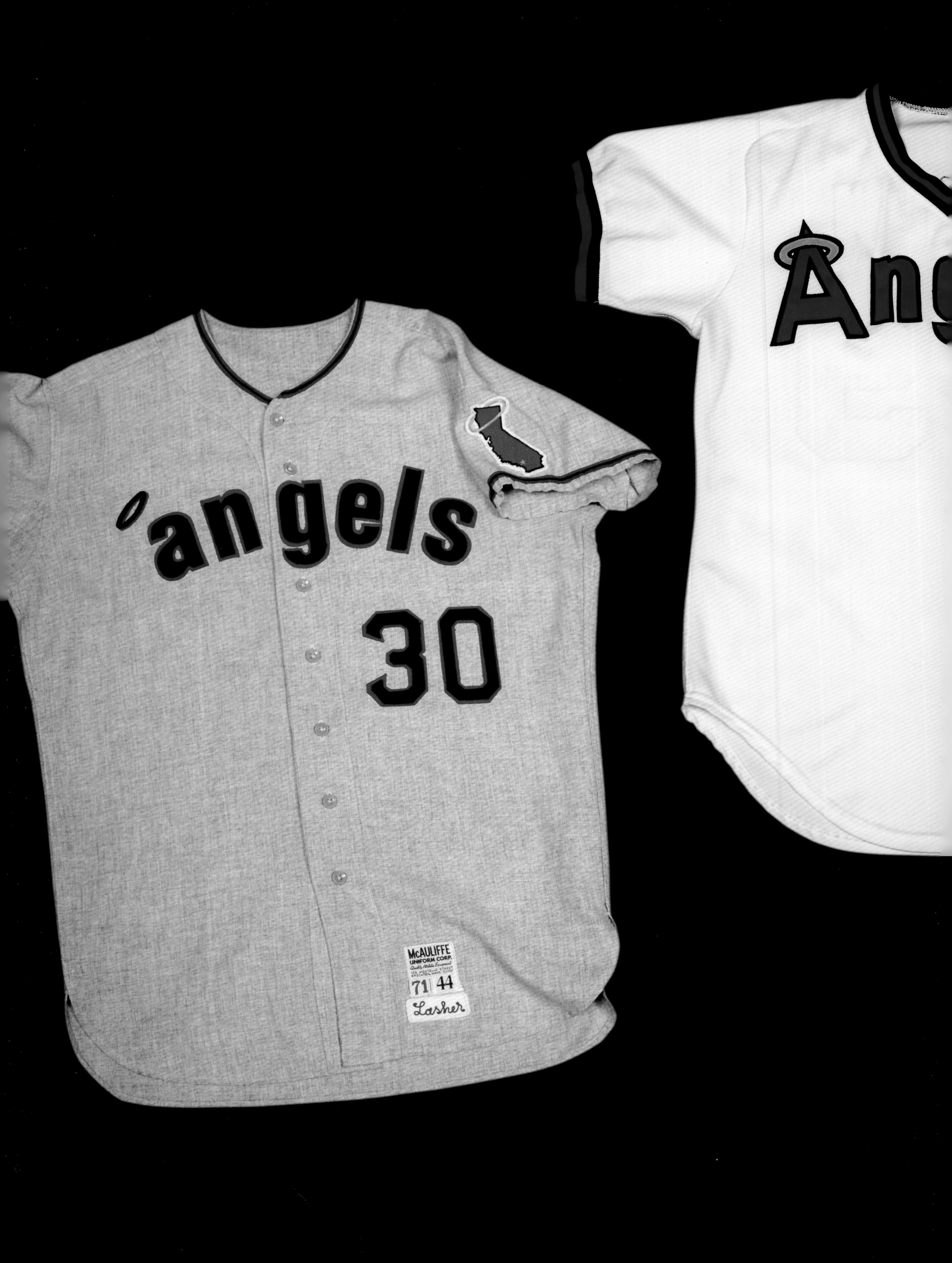
'angels
30
McAULIFFE
UNIFORM CORP.
71 44
Lasher
Ang

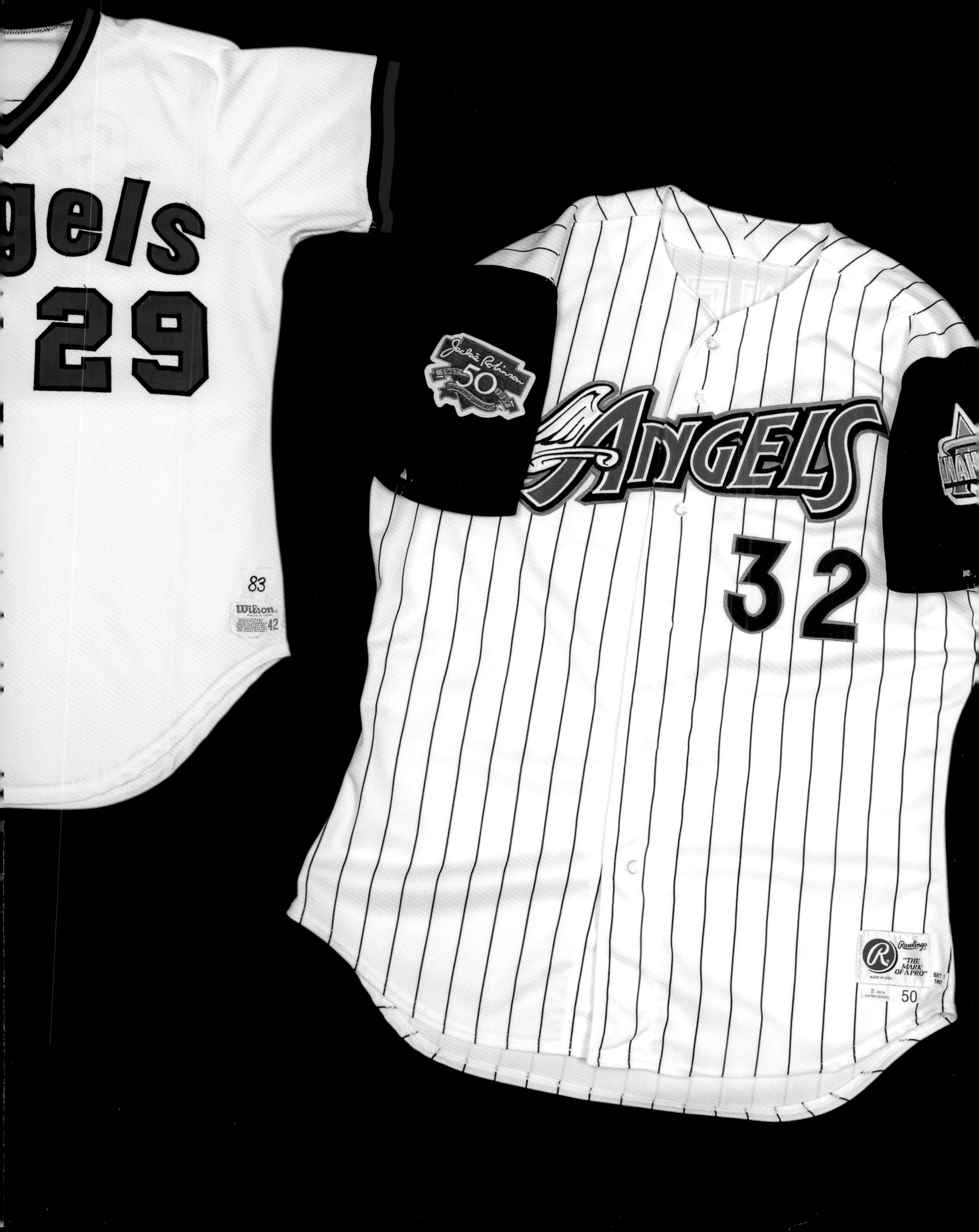
gels
29
83
Wilson
42
ANGELS
32
Rawlings
"THE MARK OF A PRO"
50

CONTENTS

CHAPTER 3: 1980s

MAUCH AND MEMORIES 109

CHAPTER 4: 1990s

CHANGING TIMES 153

CHAPTER 5: 2000s

CHAMPIONS 187

FOREWORD

BY TIM SALMON

I will never forget the feeling I got the first time I put on an Angels uniform. It was in extended Spring Training, and I felt as if I was walking into a dream world. The Angels wore red spikes in those days, and from the first time I put them on, I knew I was a part of something that was big and exciting. What I didn't know is that the Angels organization would become a second family to me.

When I first came up to the big leagues, Gene Autry owned the team, and he was always coming down to the clubhouse to talk with the players. Mr. Autry was very nice to me, but more than anything, I'll never forget the way he treated my family.

One day, when Mr. Autry was in the clubhouse, I told him that my dad had a big collection of his comic books from when he was a kid. His eyes lit up, and he said, "Bring your dad out to a game. And make sure he brings those comic books." A few nights later, I brought my dad to Mr. Autry's box, and they went through all the comic books together. Mr. Autry told my dad stories about each and every one of them, and my dad couldn't have been more thrilled. Because my dad was so excited to spend time with his childhood hero, I was excited, too.

When the Walt Disney company bought the team from Mr. Autry, no one knew what to expect, but it turned out to be a very exciting time. Being employees, we all got Silver Passes and could go to Disneyland whenever we wanted. There was talk about a monorail connecting Disneyland to the stadium someday. When I told my kids that Mickey Mouse was my boss, they loved it. We won a World Series under Disney's ownership, so it turned out to be a magical time.

Left Fan favorite Tim Salmon acknowledges the Angel Stadium crowd during his final weekend as an active player.

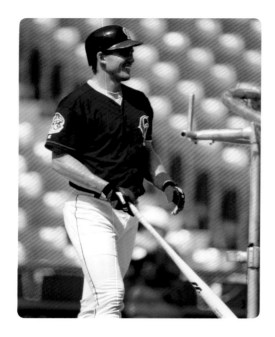

By the time we won that World Series, Troy Percival and I were the longest-tenured guys on the team, and because we had been through some of the lean times, it meant a lot more to us to win with the Angels than it would have meant anywhere else.

People always remember how good the World Series team was, but we had really good teams in the mid-1990s, too. When I look back on my career with the Angels, I think of those years as always being competitive. That said, I knew the Angels have had a lot of heartache over the years.

When I first came up in 1992, we were rebuilding, and I heard a lot of stories about players from the old days. I would talk to longtime staffers like Ned Bergert and Rick Smith about what happened here in the past, what the players were like, and how it felt to be within one game of the World Series in both '82 and '86, only to come up short. When we finally won the Series in 2002, I felt we

had put those demons to rest for everyone who had ever been a part of the organization. We also eased the pain for our loyal fans, and that meant a lot to me. Because I spent so many years with the Angels and was always treated so well by those fans, I have always felt a special connection to them.

I played for the Angels from the cradle to the grave, and staying with the Angels for my entire career was important to me. Part of it goes back to the generation in which I grew up. It was meaningful for guys like Cal Ripken and Don Mattingly to play on the same team throughout their careers, and I wanted to do the same.

While spending my entire career in the Angels organization is a highlight for me, I feel a little awkward when people call me Mr. Angel. There have been so many great players in the history of the franchise, and to be singled out somehow does not seem right to me.

Top Left Countless hours in the batting cage enabled Salmon to become the Angels' career leader in home runs (299).

Top Right Salmon waves to the Angels' fans as the team departs for their 2002 AL Division Series against the New York Yankees.

Left Stars of the 2002 World Series Champion Angels line the field: (from left) 2B Adam Kennedy, 1B Scott Spiezio, 3B Troy Glaus, LF Garret Anderson, RF Tim Salmon, CF Darin Erstad, SS David Eckstein, and Manager Mike Scioscia.

I am pleased to be remembered as someone who always went about things the right way and conducted himself in a manner that made the organization proud. The Angels always approached things the same way, and I think that's why we have had such a long association.

I'll never forget what Joe Maddon told us my first year in the Instructional League. "You are the guys who will change the face of the organization," he said. "You have to believe you're the foundation for the Angels' first world championship!"

Joe was right, and over the course of my career, I saw the development of the organization. When Arte Moreno took over in 2003, he brought the wherewithal to put a competitive team on the field every year and completed the Angels'

transformation into a marquee franchise. We went from being considered a small-market team to being a large-market team, playing with the big boys.

Now that I have been retired for five years, I have a much better perspective on how far the franchise has come and how much my time with the Angels means to me. You always want to leave a positive mark wherever you've been. One of the things I am most proud of is that the Angels were better when I left than they were when I first arrived.

From that first day in extended Spring Training, when I put on those red spikes, to the day I hung up a pair of black ones, the Angels have been like family to me. Every time I go back to Angel Stadium, I am going home.

Above Fans show their appreciation for Salmon during his last game on October 1, 2006.

>>

I'll never forget what Joe Maddon told us my first year in the Instructional League. "You are the guys who will change the face of the organization," he said. "You have to believe you're the foundation for the Angels' first world championship!"

>>

PREFACE

BY ARTE MORENO

Baseball has always been a big part of my life; I have loved the game since I was young. The late John Wooden had a saying, both simple and powerful, that summarizes my lifelong dedication to the game: "Passion is short-term, love is long-term." To me, this great game is part of the American culture, and it is part of life.

The excitement of watching some of my favorite players, such as Hank Aaron, Roberto Clemente, and Rod Carew, remains fresh in my mind. I have a great deal of respect and admiration for those who compete at a higher level in baseball—particularly those whose skills lead to individual accomplishment and team success.

Though I have shared in ownership on the minor league (Salt Lake City Trappers) and major league levels (Arizona Diamondbacks), purchasing the Angels in May 2003 has been one of my most satisfying and rewarding experiences. This franchise has provided our fan base numerous memorable moments since its inception in 1961. There

are the individual milestones: Rod Carew's 3,000th hit, American League MVP honors for Don Baylor and Vladimir Guerrero, Cy Young awards for Dean Chance and Bartolo Colon, Reggie Jackson's 500th home run, Don Sutton's 300th win, the four no-hitters by Nolan Ryan, a perfect game by Mike Witt, and Mike Scioscia's 1,000th career win, to name a few. Then there are organizational highlights, such as hosting three All-Star Games, clinching eight division titles, and, of course, winning a World Championship in 2002.

It has given all of us within the Angels family a great sense of pride to watch the continued growth of the organization, both on the field and within our

"We have dedicated ourselves to becoming perennial contenders during the season and difference-makers within our community year-round, as we feel it is equally important to invest in our community as it is to compete at the highest level to win a championship."　—ARTE MORENO

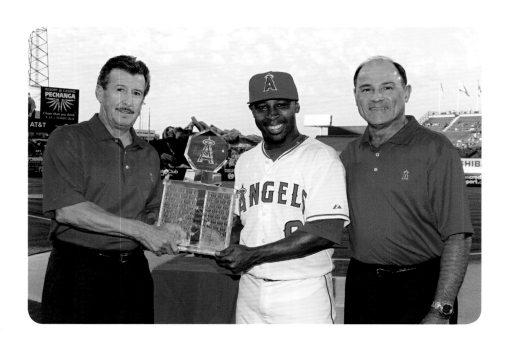

Top Left Owner Arte Moreno presents Chone Figgins with an award for breaking team record for stolen bases with 187. He would finish his Angels career with 280.

Top Right and Right Moreno is always quick with a smile for players and fans.

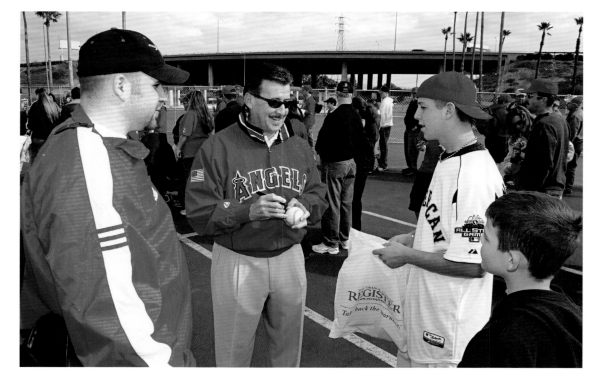

community, as well as the growth of our reputation on a national level. We have dedicated ourselves to becoming perennial contenders during the season and difference-makers within our community year-round, as we feel it is equally important to invest in our community as it is to compete at the highest level to win a championship.

The Angel brand has become synonymous with quality play, affordability, and the ballpark experience, all of which remain the focus and objective of those who proudly wear the red "A." We will strive to excel in each of these categories for years to come, and it is a responsibility we embrace on a daily basis.

Along the way, the organization has been embraced by a loyal fan base, and that legion has grown in recent years, resulting in an annual home attendance of over three million per season since 2003! Our priority remains our fans.

This publication has afforded us the opportunity to reflect on the past, as well as look with excitement to the future. In the pages that follow, I hope you enjoy the story and journey of Angels Baseball. Thank you for being an Angel fan, and Go Angels!

Above Moreno congratulates his team for winning the West Division title on September 28, 2009.

INTRODUCTION

BY MIKE SCIOSCIA

Everyone associated with the Angels organization is extremely proud to be a part of the history of the team. During my 12 seasons in the Angels dugout, I have always taken great pride in being able to build on the foundation that was established by those who preceded me.

One of the organization's goals has always been to have a philosophy and a staff in place throughout our system that enables us to develop championship-caliber players and play championship-caliber baseball. In order to meet that standard, everyone must be relentless, and this is a dynamic outfit that does not sit back and rest on its laurels.

When Arte Moreno took over as the club's owner in 2003, he gave us the resources to compete at a very high level, year in and year out. Arte puts his money where his mouth is, and his leadership has enabled us to field a competitive team each and every season.

We have also worked hard to make the Angels organization feel like an extended family. We try to create an atmosphere that enables players and staff members to feel comfortable.

Our fans are also an important part of our family unit and have helped make Angel Stadium a special place to play baseball. Any time you show up to Angel Stadium as a player or a manager, you know there will be at least 40,000 fans there, supporting you. Angel Stadium provides a great backdrop for baseball, and it has developed into a favorite ballpark, not only for our ballplayers but for opposing players, too. Everyone knows the ambience is going to be great, and that makes it conducive to going out and playing good baseball.

Over the course of my 12 seasons here, we have striven to implement philosophies that we believe will bring championship-caliber play. We teach an aggressive brand of baseball and expect our players to bring that style of play onto the field each and every day.

Above The Angels have welcomed over 3 million fans each season since 2003.

Left Throughout their history, the Angels have shared a special relationship with their fans, as evidenced by Wally Joyner's popularity in 1986.

Our fans are also an important part of our family unit and have helped make Angel Stadium a special place to play baseball. Any time you show up to Angel Stadium as a player or a manager, you know there will be at least 40,000 fans there, supporting you.

The pages of this book are devoted to the people who have helped shape this organization into a perennial contender, from Gene Autry to Arte Moreno, from Jim Fregosi to Torii Hunter. Inside, you will find stories about memorable personalities and see images culled from a photo vault of Angels history. Many of the pictures inside this book have never been published before.

Everyone who has been associated with the franchise over the years has worked hard to build an organization of which our fans can be proud, and I think this book depicts the level of pride everyone within the organization feels for Angels baseball. I hope you enjoy reliving Angels history through this book as much as I have enjoyed being a part of it.

From their embryonic and modest beginnings, from a long love affair between an almost-accidental owner and his players, from a collection of cast-offs who wove a fabric of unequaled camaraderie into a team, the Angels as we know them today were born. With superstars, surprise heroes, roaring crowds, and regular playoff appearances, they have emerged as one of the prominent forces in America's pastime, a model franchise with a rich history of triumph, tragedy, togetherness, and titles.

THIS IS THEIR STORY.

CHAPTER I: 1960s

THE BIRTH OF THE ANGELS

Gene Autry, "the Singing Cowboy" and lifelong baseball fan.

By the time he arrived in St. Louis in December of 1960 for baseball's Winter Meetings, Gene Autry was one of the best-known entertainers in the country.

He was a megastar on radio, in the movies, on television, and in the recording industry. He had recorded some 635 songs, been on radio for 16 years and television for 6, and made 95 films.

The 53-year-old Autry was also a shrewd and successful businessman who had accumulated a financial empire that included 10 radio stations under the name Golden West Broadcasting. He was in St. Louis in an attempt to obtain the broadcast rights for the new American League expansion team in Los Angeles for his radio station, KMPC.

The team in question was facing some initial obstacles, however: Dodgers owner Walter O'Malley blocked the team's proposed ownership by a group that included maverick Bill Veeck, so American League president Joe Cronin turned to Autry and asked him to bid on the team. Autry agreed and, after purchasing the name from O'Malley (who had bought it in 1957 from chewing gum magnate William Wrigley Jr. in anticipation of moving his team from Brooklyn to California) for $350,000, the Angels were born.

O'Malley initially objected to an American League team in Los Angeles until 1962, when Dodger Stadium would be completed, but after meetings with the affable Autry and the general manager of Autry's radio station, Bob Reynolds, the Dodgers owner relented. "Gene Autry and Bob Reynolds are the kind of people that will be good for the game. We are delighted that they have been awarded a franchise. I hope the Angels can bring an American League pennant to Los Angeles very soon," said O'Malley.

Autry was ecstatic: "We are overwhelmed by the news," he said. "And we're ready to roll." Well, not quite ready, as it turned out.

"In the beginning," Autry said, "we didn't have any players, baseballs, or bats. In fact, we didn't have a stadium." Autry, along with Reynolds, the onetime Stanford All-American tackle who would be the president of the team, immediately went to work and hired former Milwaukee Braves manager Fred Haney (who attended the meeting in St. Louis in hopes of getting the broadcast job if Autry got the rights) to be general manager, and, in turn, Haney promptly hired former Giants manager Bill Rigney to manage the club. Longtime Major League Baseball manager Casey Stengel, who was between

"Gene Autry and Bob Reynolds are the kind of people that will be good for the game. We are delighted that they have been awarded a franchise. I hope the Angels can bring an American League pennant to Los Angeles very soon," said O'Malley.

jobs, was rumored to be the first choice, but he had secretly agreed to a deal to manage the expansion Mets the following year, making Rigney an easy and popular choice.

Days later, an expansion draft was held, and the Angels selected a total of 30 players from the available pool. The kaleidoscope roster included veterans like Eddie Yost, Eli Grba, and Ted Kluszewski and youngsters Bob Rodgers, Dean Chance, Ken McBride, and Jim Fregosi, a 19-year-old shortstop from the Red Sox. The Angels paid a total of $2,150,000 for their first roster ($75,000 per player).

And so, with Autry leading the way, a pair of veterans in the front office and in the dugout, and a potpourri of players, the Angels took their place in the American League. For the Cowboy, it was to be a love affair that never ended.

It had been a breathtaking month, from ownership to management to team in less than 30 days. The Angels would prove to be the most successful in expansion history, winning 70 games that first year of 1961 and contending for the pennant the following season before finishing third.

The Angels had a front office and a team. Next, they needed a home. They rented Wrigley Field in downtown Los Angeles for their inaugural season. Named after William Wrigley Jr. (who owned the Los Angeles Angels before O'Malley purchased them), the stadium in south-central L.A., on the corner of 42nd and Avalon, had a rich history but a capacity of only 20,000. The minor league Angels—and the Hollywood Stars for a time—had played their home games at Wrigley from 1925 to 1957. A year later, the Angels would move into the new Dodger Stadium in Chavez Ravine (the Angels

Top Left Gene Autry, first Angels president Bob Reynolds, and Dodgers owner Walter O'Malley.

Left Autry and his first manager, Bill Rigney, had roughly three months to fast-track the building of the Angels organization.

Above First Angels president Reynolds, first Angels general manager Fred Haney, and Autry.

Above Pitchers Ryne Duren, Art Fowler, and Tom Morgan were part of the original Angels staff.

organization referred to the location as Chavez Ravine Stadium), where they played for the next four seasons before finding a permanent home in Anaheim in 1966. They paid O'Malley $200,000 per year, or 7.5 percent of the gate receipts, to use the new park.

The club also selected Palm Springs for their Spring Training home. They set up shop at the old Desert Inn and played at the Polo Grounds. Autry would go on to buy his own hotel in town, and today is considered one of the pioneers of this glittering desert community. Tributes include a street named after the Cowboy and a prominent statue downtown.

Palm Springs, just 100 miles from Los Angeles, was a destination for Hollywood luminaries, and the new Angels fit right in. Rigney would hold court with "his writers," while the players found the warm spring days and pleasing nightlife to their liking.

"It was something in those days," Chance said. Dick Enberg, who would become the voice of the Angels, recalled, "It was a four-week Mardi Gras in this chic resort mecca."

Pedalling the streets of Palm Springs, the Angels' Spring Training home, circa 1961.

Q&A with ALBIE PEARSON

ON JOINING THE ANGELS . . .

I was quite small, to say the least. I never grew up. I can remember, at 12 years old, being four feet four inches and weighing 64 pounds or so. The odds of me ever even having a chance to play baseball were just impossible. Or so it seemed.

After I had my Rookie of the Year season with the Washington Senators, I got a back injury and could not find a team that would have me. But I knew I still had talent and that I still wanted to play, so I wrote a letter to Fred Haney and asked him to select me in the expansion draft. I ended up as the 28th player drafted, and I wore the number 28 for all my years with the Angels.

ON HIS ROLE AS LEADOFF HITTER . . .

As a leadoff man with the Angels, my job was to try to get on base. Just get on base anyway I could and get the hole open between first and second and get a guy working out of a stretch with maybe a little less in his fastball for our next batter. I could create some havoc over there and start some rallies, and that's what I wanted to do. That was always my thought when I got in the batter's box. Whenever I came up to bat, somebody in the dugout would say "Hey, Little Man, get us started, man, get us started," and I would be grinding up there trying to get a walk, get hit in the ribs, base hit, bunt, whatever I could get.

ON JIM FREGOSI . . .

He had real talent. He was a battler, and he played really hard. He had enough voice in the clubhouse and on the field to have the guys all look to him as the leader. He was a good ballplayer, but what made him really solid was his capability as a leader. He talked, but more important, he lived and worked hard in front of everybody. Everybody caught hold of that good example.

ON AN EARLY ANGELS FAN . . .

One of my first memories from our first team, to go back to '61, was President Eisenhower watching us play in Palm Springs. The president and Uncle Gene—I always called [Autry] that—were quite close friends, and the president was an Angels fan right from the beginning. Uncle Gene asked us all to sign a bat to give to President Eisenhower as a gift, a gift for our first number one fan. I got to take it over to the country club where he lived, and I gave it to him on the putting green. He absolutely looked at it like it was the greatest thing that had ever been placed in his hands. And it was just a bat signed by a bunch of young kids, but it was still special to him. I had a chance to play a little golf with him that day, and I will never forget it.

ON DAVID ECHSTEIN . . .

David is a giant compared to me. I had a chance to shake his hand and let him know that he is such a great player. David is an overachiever, a winner. He is the kind of player who knew how to handle situations. He was the fireplug for the 2002 team.

Below The inaugural Angels game at Wrigley Field in Los Angeles.

"The newness, the magic of opening day, fearing the worst and getting the best, there are just not many days that golden," Autry recalled in his autobiography, *Back in the Saddle Again.* **The Angels were off and running.**

》》》》》》》》》》》》》》》》》》》》》》》》》》》》》》》》》》》》》》》

On March 1, 1961, the Angels played their first Spring Training game. President Eisenhower, who had just left office in January and had a home in nearby Rancho Mirage, was a guest in the dugout before the first pitch. He posed for pictures with Kluszewski and big Steve Bilko, saying they could play for George Halas's Chicago Bears in the National Football League.

On opening day, April 11, Kluszewski, the thick slugger from Cincinnati, homered twice, and Grba, who couldn't crack the rotation in New York, pitched a complete game for the win, 7–2. Autry called the opening victory the greatest thrill of his career—this after he owned the team for 38 years. "The newness, the magic of opening day, fearing the worst and getting the best, there are just not many days that golden," Autry recalled in his autobiography, *Back in the Saddle Again.* The Angels were off and running.

On April 27, 1961, a crowd of 11,931 showed up at Wrigley, some paying as much as $3.50 for a box seat, to see Ty Cobb throw out the first pitch and the Minnesota Twins down the home team, 4–2. Wrigley would prove to be a power paradise, with a record 248 home runs launched during the season, a record that would stand for 30 years.

Kluszewski, Grba, and others contributed, but it was the young players like Fregosi, Chance, Rodgers, McBride, and Albie Pearson who emerged as the stalwarts of the '60s.

Fregosi would become the face of the franchise for more than a decade; Chance would win a Cy Young with a remarkable 1964 season; Rodgers would catch over 900 games for the team; McBride led the first team with a dozen wins; and Pearson, the popular "Little Angel" at five feet five, was an All-Star by 1963. Fregosi and Rodgers would both go on to manage the team years later.

"We had so much fun in those days," said Fregosi. "I was fortunate to come up to the majors at 19 and learned so much from veterans like Rocky Bridges and Del Rice and Eddie Yost and, of course, Rig, who taught me to love the game and to stay in it after my playing days, which I did."

Haney and Rigney were brilliant in their respective roles. Haney plucked players like Leon Wagner and Lee Thomas from other clubs. The two sluggers would combine for 53 home runs that first season. Rigney was a genius at blending a team with castoffs and kids.

After winning 70 games that first season, the Angels caught the league by surprise in '62, leading the chase for the pennant as late as the Fourth of July. They would finish in third place with 86 wins, and Rigney was named the American League Manager of the Year. "Anybody who played on that team back in '62," said Chance, who was 14-10 as a 21-year-old, "will tell you it was the greatest Angels season ever. We had so much fun, and we were in the race all season."

Left The quintessential Angel, Jim Fregosi.

Top Right Pitchers Ken McBride, Dean Chance, and Bo Belinsky.

Right Leadoff hitter Albie Pearson is flanked by Ted Kluszewski and Steve Bilko.

ANGELS

CORPORATION

SOI

Q&A with BUCK RODGERS

ON THE 1962 ANGELS . . .

We were in first place on the Fourth of July, with this ragtag bunch, but Bill Rigney was a magician in finding out what guys cannot do. That's one thing he told me and Fregosi—he always talked to us like we were going to be managers, like he knew that—he said, the biggest thing about managing is finding out what a guy cannot do, and then don't let him do it. We had platoon players, we had bullpen by committee, and all those things meshed into a ball club, so pretty soon we said, "You know, we're pretty good."

ON DEAN CHANCE . . .

I got to know him well, catching him all those years. It was very intimidating waiting for one of his pitches. Basically, he had only two pitches: a fastball and a breaking pitch, either a slider or a curveball, depending on the day. His delivery was so deceptive, the way he turned his back. Dean took every pitch I called seriously, and he was a fiery competitor who had great stuff.

ON BOBBY KNOOP . . .

Pitchers loved Bobby Knoop because pitchers loved double plays, and Bobby could make double plays. He was a great fielder who could field the ball that just got by the pitcher and stick his nose in the ground. Many times, his forehead would hit the ground on difficult plays.

ON JIM FREGOSI . . .

The one thing I loved about Jimmy, as a catcher, was that if I made an errant throw to second, he would stick his nose right into the play, make the catch, and make the tag. He was an outstanding shortstop.

ON GENE AUTRY . . .

He was our biggest fan. He would sit with us and talk for hours about the old days. He knew players, and he knew stats. He always made it a point to come in to the clubhouse, whether we won or lost. He would come down and sit with us, and we'd kid each other.

ON ALBIE PEARSON . . .

He stood five five and three-eighths. We never called him just five five because he would always let you know about those three-eighths. He was a good player and a good center fielder. He ran the bases well, and he was a good leadoff man, an excellent leadoff man. And he had some pop in his bat.

ON THE ANGELS UNIFORM . . .

I loved those hats we wore . . . you saw just a little bit of that halo, and you knew, there's an Angel.

Above Slugger Steve Bilko and teammates Ken Hunt, Earl Averill, Leon Wagner, and Lee Thomas.

"Anybody who played on that team back in '62," said Chance, who was 14-10 as a 21-year-old, "will tell you it was the greatest Angel season ever. We had so much fun, and we were in the race all season."

One of the players on that team was Leon "Daddy Wags" Wagner, another colorful character in the cast. A sharp dresser who owned a clothing store, Wagner had a banner campaign, hitting 37 homers, driving in 107 runs, and being named Most Valuable Player of the second summer All-Star Game when he collected three hits, including a two-run home run.

The 1962 season will also be remembered for the debut of one Robert Belinsky, a former pool hustler and man-about-town from New York whom the Angels drafted out of the Orioles organization the previous winter. A left-handed pitcher, Bo Belinsky was a charismatic playboy who gained celebrity by dating a long list of Hollywood starlets. But on the night of May 5, he pitched his way into the record book and Angels history by tossing a no-hitter against Baltimore. It was his fifth straight win and the first no-hitter in Angels history. But it was also to be the highlight of Belinsky's brief career with the Angels, who traded him to Philadelphia two years later after Belinksy's altercation with an L.A. sportswriter.

Above Right Pitchers Ken McBride and Dean Chance hoped for 20 wins, a feat accomplished by Chance in 1964.

Right Bo Belinsky made headlines on and off the field.

Above Leon "Daddy Wags" Wagner.

Left Ever the celebrity, Belinsky hobnobs with Dean Martin and Henry Fonda.

MAY 5, 1962

BO BELINSKY TOSSES FIRST NO-HITTER IN ANGELS HISTORY

★★

Chavez Ravine, Los Angeles

Bo Belinsky, the Angels' charismatic playboy and talented left-handed pitcher, became the first pitcher in club history to throw a no-hitter when he blanked the Baltimore Orioles, 2–0. The win put the Angels over the .500 mark at 10-9, and they never were under .500 the remainder of the season.

Belinsky struck out the first two Orioles in the first inning, but a walk and a hit batter put him in a jam in the second. He escaped, however, thanks to a groundout and another strikeout. In the fourth, the Orioles loaded the bases with one out following two walks and an error by third baseman Felix Torres. But Belinsky struck out Dave Nicholson, and Ron Hansen flew out to deep center field to end the inning.

Meanwhile, the Angels pushed across single runs in the first and second but were held to only three hits of their own for the next six innings. Belinsky got stronger and retired 12 of 13 Orioles heading into the ninth.

Jackie Brandt struck out to start the inning, Belinsky's ninth and final strikeout of the game. Gus Triandos grounded out to Joe Koppe at short, setting up the final showdown with Nicholson, who'd struck out twice. Nicholson popped out to Torres in foul territory, and Belinsky made history, throwing not only the first Angels no-hitter but also the first at newly built Dodger Stadium.

Belinsky won his next start to begin his career 5-0, and on June 21, the 25-year-old lefty was 7-2, with a splendid 2.90 ERA.

Q&A with DEAN CHANCE

ON HIS WINDUP . . .

I turned my back on the batter. That was just my natural way of pitching, and I never saw too good out of my left eye, so if I'd have tried to stay and watch, I probably wouldn't have had as good of control as I had. Believe me, I did not have good control. I had to fight all the time to get the ball around. I was fortunate that I threw it with the seams that sank. In '64, when I won the Cy Young Award, I only gave up seven home runs, which was unreal when you lead the league in innings pitched, but that old stadium was a tremendous place for a pitcher.

ON HIS DEFENSE . . .

I got a lot of breaks from Bobby Knoop and Jim Fregosi. One game, I was winning 1–0 against Minnesota, and they had runners on first and third with one out, and Jimmie Hall hit a line shot to second, and somehow Knoop went way to his right, backhanded the ball with his left hand, flipped it to Fregosi, and they got a double play. Otherwise it would have been runners on first and third, and the score would have been tied 1–1. Those two guys were unreal that year, because it's an inch here and an inch there—that's the difference between winning and losing. They helped me win 20 games in '64. That year they meant a lot, and it was just my year because I got the breaks and won 15 games the second half of the season.

ON JIM FREGOSI . . .

Jimmy put out 100 percent at all times. He ran—he could really run, too—and he gave 100 percent. I can't say enough about what he did in '62. I had a terrible move to first; I couldn't hold anybody on. I did have a good move to second, but Fregosi was the key because he had to break there, and it was a timing play. Jimmy had the knack, the ability as a shortstop, to time it perfectly. So when I saw daylight between him and the runner, I would lead him to the bag with my throw.

ON BO BELINSKY'S NO-HITTER . . .

Bo's no-hitter stands out the most in my memory of the early team. Everybody on that team remembers the no-hitter that day because it made the headlines and it was really a shot in the arm for us. Bo had good stuff, a good fastball, and that night everything worked. Bo and I were both pitchers from the Orioles organization, so we knew each other pretty well. Anybody that knew Bo Belinsky liked him. If he lost, he did not get that mad or say anything.

ON BILL RIGNEY . . .

Bill Rigney—"Rig," we called him—had his hands full with us young kids. But he was tremendous. He played hunches; he knew his players. All he could do was give me the ball, and I knew I had to do the rest from the mound. He gave me the ball and let me work, so I have nothing but praise for him.

1964 DEAN CHANCE'S CY YOUNG SEASON

★★

Dean Chance, only 23 years old and in just his third full major league season, dominated the American League throughout the spring and summer to win the Cy Young Award, at a time when only one Cy Young was awarded. (Each league began issuing their own Cy Young beginning in 1967.)

Chance, a self-proclaimed farm boy from Ohio, was only 5-5 at the All-Star break in July, but sported a minuscule 2.19 ERA, good enough to earn the start in the Midsummer Classic, where he pitched three scoreless innings.

In the second half, Chance won nine straight games from July 11 through August 18, six of them shutouts, and four of those by a 1–0 score. During the streak, he allowed only seven earned runs in 79 innings (0.80 ERA).

His brilliance was perhaps best illustrated by his complete dominance of the New York Yankees. Chance pitched five games against them, posting a 4-0 record. In 50 innings of work against New York, Chance allowed one run, a solo home run by Mickey Mantle, who called Chance the toughest pitcher he ever faced.

Chance finished with a 20-9 record and an eye-popping 1.65 ERA. He threw 11 shutouts, five of them by a 1–0 score. (He also lost four games, 1–0.)

Of the 278 1/3 innings Chance pitched in 1964, opponents scored in only 35 of them. The other 243 1/3 were scoreless!

Above Construction of the stadium began in 1964 and continued until 1966, when the Angels moved into a home of their own.

While Belinsky's star rose and faded rather quickly, Dean Chance's was shining brighter than ever by 1964. A strapping farm boy from Ohio, Chance had a wicked delivery in which he nearly turned his back to home plate and delivered rising and sinking fastballs. Few pitchers in the game have had a season like Chance did that year. Not only did he win 20 games (20-9), but he had a major-league-best ERA of 1.65, completed 15 games with 11 shutouts (5 were by the score of 1–0), struck out 207, and won the Cy Young Award (which in those days was for both leagues).

Meanwhile, the Angels were looking for a stadium they could call their own. The city of Anaheim, a burgeoning tourist destination with the completion of Disneyland in 1955, came calling. The city proposed building a 43,000-capacity state-of-the-art stadium on 140 acres of agricultural land, just minutes from Disneyland. (It likely helped that Walt Disney was on the Angels' advisory board.) The Angels agreed, breaking ground in 1964, and the team was on the move for the last time. (The two entertainment entities would partner many times through the years. In 1967, a promotional package for an Angels ticket and admission to Disneyland and access to all rides was sold for $5).

In '65, the Angels, in anticipation of the move to Anaheim, changed the name of the team from the Los Angeles Angels to the California Angels.

The new stadium opened in 1966 and featured a 230-foot-high scoreboard shaped like an A (hence the stadium's nickname, the Big A). It has stood as an Orange County landmark for more than 40 years, a symbol of the arrival of the major leagues. The halo atop the Big A is lit after every Angels victory, home and away.

The Angels' home circa 1980.

Above Dean Chance and Jim Fregosi became stars under the Halo.

Right Shortstop Fregosi and second baseman Bobby Knoop formed one of the American League's premier double-play tandems.

Far Right Four-time team MVP Bobby Knoop "turns two."

The new stadium opened in 1966 and featured a 230-foot-high scoreboard, shaped like an "A." Hence, the stadium's nickname, the "Big A." It has stood as an Orange County landmark for more than 40 years, a symbol of the arrival of the major leagues. The halo atop the Big A is lighted after every Angel victory, home and away.

The move proved to be a financial success. In their last season at Chavez Ravine, the Angels had averaged only 6,997 fans per game. In 1966, in their new Orange County home, the Angels drew 1.4 million fans, an average of 17,288 per game.

Dean Chance's spectacular season and the start of construction of the Big A were just two of the big stories of 1964. That same year, Bobby Knoop, who had been drafted out of the Braves organization, took over at second base, where he would win three Gold Gloves over the next five seasons, teaming with the emerging Fregosi to form one of the games' best double-play combinations. And in June '64, the Angels won a bidding war for a superb two-sport star from the University of Wisconsin, Rick Reichardt. The Angels paid a record $200,000 for the phenom, who would hit the first regular-season home run at the new Anaheim Stadium in 1966. (Willie Mays hit the first homer, in a Spring Training game that year).

In 1965, the club obtained another player who was to be an Angels icon. In the sixth round of the major league draft, they chose Clyde Wright from Carson-Newman College in Tennessee. Wright would pitch a no-hitter for the team, win 22 games in one season, and become a fixture at Anaheim Stadium in a variety of roles for the next 40-plus seasons.

After Wright's major league debut in '66, a four-hitter against the Twins, Angels trainer Freddie Frederico decided to call the lefty Skeeter. "He told me," said Wright, "that no big leaguer should be called Clyde. And the name stuck."

But the centerpiece of the team throughout the later part of the '60s was their shortstop, Fregosi, a handsome Italian from San Mateo's fabled Junipero Serra High School. A favorite of Autry's, Fregosi played the game in textbook fashion. He didn't posses great power or blazing speed, but he had all the inherent instincts of a star. Game after game, year after year, he was out there at short, making plays, positioning teammates, counseling pitchers. He became an All-Star during that '64 season and was chosen to the American League squad five more times.

Fregosi was a catalyst for a scrappy 1967 team that contended for much of the year. In July, the Angels hosted their first All-Star Game, with Fregosi, pitcher Jim McGlothlin, and first baseman Don Mincher (acquired in a trade for Chance) all making the team. A seven-game winning streak after the All-Star contest (won by the National League when Tony Perez of the Reds homered in the 15th inning) propelled the Angels to third place, 10 games over .500. The team finished a solid 84-77 with reliever Minnie Rojas saving 27 games, Mincher hitting 25 home runs, and Fregosi and Knoop playing wonderfully in the infield.

Left Gene Autry presents Fregosi, one of his favorite players, with the Owner's Trophy in 1963.

Q&A with JACKIE AUTRY

ON THE EARLY ANGELS . . .

I was a banker in Palm Springs, and I met Gene when he was buying his hotel there in the '80s. But I can remember the Angels from the earliest days of the 1960s, all the players riding down Palm Canyon Drive on bicycles. I suppose they rode because they didn't have the financial wherewithal to rent limousines, especially since they had a franchise in which they had no bats, balls, or gloves. I saw so many Angels games in those days.

ON HER FAVORITE EARLY PLAYERS . . .

In those early days, my favorite player was Ted Kluszewski, only because he was such a big guy. And I also liked Jim Fregosi a lot; he was a wonderful shortstop. And Albie Pearson, I liked him, so there were a lot of good guys on that ball club. I remember the first game they played; it was in Baltimore, and Ted Kluszewski hit a home run, and they won that game, and Gene said that was the happiest moment of his life.

ON GENE AUTRY . . .

It was hard not to be impressed with Gene. He was well dressed. He was a very sweet, gentle person. He had an extraordinary sense of humor. His greatest strength as an owner was surrounding himself with good people and letting them run the business. He also loved his players and treated them like a family. The fellows all felt like a unit; they all admired Gene, not for what he did in the past, but for what he did as an owner. They knew that he cared.

ON HER BEST MEMORY OF GENE AUTRY AS OWNER OF THE ANGELS . . .

This may sound strange, but I would have to say the 2002 World Series, because I felt Gene's presence all the time. I saw the fans in the stands holding signs that said, WIN ONE FOR THE COWBOY. I could feel his presence all over, and I just got chills.

ON REGGIE JACKSON . . .

He had a style about him. That style transcended to the other ballplayers on our club and helped us win in '82. Reggie put fans in the stands and added a lot to the clubhouse.

ON GENE MAUCH . . .

He was my favorite manager to work with. He was an extraordinary, brilliant baseball man. There was not too much you could tell Gene about baseball.

The following year, Fred Haney retired and was replaced by Dick Walsh, and in the spring of '69, Walsh fired Rigney after a poor start and hired Lefty Phillips to run the team.

Haney had served as general manager for eight seasons (1961–1968), had seen two Angels teams ('62 and '67) compete for the pennant, and was instrumental in the acquisition of virtually all the players who played under the Halo in its first decade. Rigney, as popular with the media as he was with his players, guided the team to 625 wins, some of them improbable and many of them memorable.

The Angels would eventually retire Fregosi's No. 11 and No. 26, symbolic of their 26th man, the owner who brought them to fruition and nurtured them through those early years, Gene Autry.

While the '60s ended with change, Autry could be proud of a great decade of baseball, but ever the competitor, he—like the rest of the team—looked forward to the promises of many seasons to come.

Top Future president Ronald Reagan poses with Bill Rigney.

Above The logo for the 1967 All-Star Game, hosted by the Angels.

Left Shay Torrent delighted Angels fans by playing the organ at home games from 1965 until his retirement in 1986.

Above Jim Fregosi's display in the Angels Hall of Fame.

CHAPTER 2: 1970s

THE EXPRESS AND
THE FIRST
CHAMPIONSHIP

On December 10, 1971, the Angels traded their most popular and productive player, Jim Fregosi, to the New York Mets for four players. Pitcher Don Rose won one game for the Angels. Pitcher Frank Estrada never got in a game. Outfielder Leroy Stanton played five years for the team and hit .247. The fourth player was a flame-throwing right-hander from Texas. His name was Nolan Ryan.

No man has been able to throw a ball as fast as Ryan, who was quickly dubbed "the Ryan Express" after the 1965 Frank Sinatra movie *Von Ryan's Express*. On nights he was scheduled to pitch in Anaheim, the crowd swelled in anticipation of another Ryan gem, one with a barrelful of strikeouts or a no-hitter. (During his career he would pitch 7 no-hitters, 12 one-hitters, and 18 two-hitters.) His fastball was once clocked at 101.9 miles per hour. Whoosh!

During his eight seasons with the Angels, Ryan led the league in strikeouts seven times, the zenith being a major-league-record 383 in 1973. He struck out more than 300 hitters five times, won more than 20 games twice, and pitched four no-hitters. And he did it all for a grand total of a million bucks. That was what he was paid for the duration of his Angels career.

As Reggie Jackson said, "Every hitter likes fastballs just like everybody likes ice cream. But you don't like it when someone's stuffing it into you by the gallon. That's how you feel when Ryan's throwing balls by you."

The formidable Nolan Ryan always gave his team a chance to win.

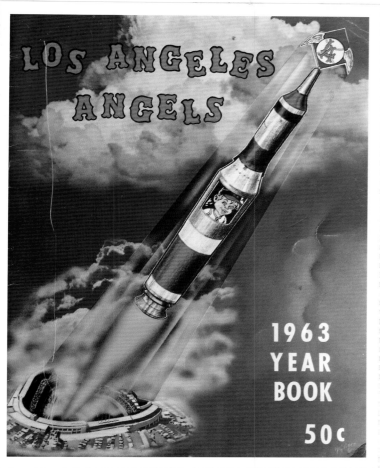

LOS ANGELES ANGELS

1963 YEAR BOOK

50¢

CALIFORNIA ANGELS PALM SPRINGS · · 1969

SAN DIEGO PADRES
OAKLAND A's
SEATTLE PILOTS

HOME OF THE ANGELS
S.F. GIANTS
CHI. CUBS
CLEVE. INDIANS

Spring Training Home
of the CALIFORNIA ANGELS

angels

OFFICIAL SCOREBOOK MAGAZINE 35¢

ANGELS

Angels

OFFICIAL SCOREBOOK MAGAZINE 40¢

RYAN EXPRESS FLAMETHROWER

the

Nolan Ryan and manager
Dave Garcia, circa 1977.

Q&A with NOLAN RYAN

ON HIS NO-HITTERS . . .

I think the Detroit no-hitter in '73 was probably the game where I had the most overpowering stuff. The game that was the most meaningful to me was my fourth no-hitter because it tied me with Sandy Koufax.

ON HIS INDUCTION INTO THE ANGELS HALL OF FAME . . .

It was very special that they honored me while I was still an active player. They did it during the season on the field, and Gene Autry was out there along with Rod Carew to make the presentation. It was a very special day, and I certainly felt honored that the Angels looked at me in that light.

ON GENE AUTRY . . .

He was very caring. He was interested in his players, and he considered them a part of his family. He accepted the wins and the losses and never got too high or too low over them. He understood the game, and I thought that he did everything as an owner to try and improve the organization and produce a winner.

ON WHAT HE CONSIDERS HIS GREATEST ACCOMPLISHMENT AS A PITCHER . . .

I think the biggest accomplishment was just having the opportunity to play as long as I did. I get a lot of satisfaction out of that because it was very unique, and very seldom does anybody get to play even 20 years in the profession. I just feel very fortunate.

ON STARTING THE 1979 ALL-STAR GAME . . .

It was very exciting and unsettling because I did not know those hitters, but I did know that all of them were All-Stars. I wanted to perform well and give my team the opportunity to win even though I was not familiar with my opponents. I think I was more nervous about it than I was over a normal start.

ON THE ANGELS WORLD SERIES VICTORY . . .

It was exciting to watch, and I was very proud of them for being able to accomplish that. I would have liked to have been in an Angels uniform when that happened. I was pulling for them the whole way.

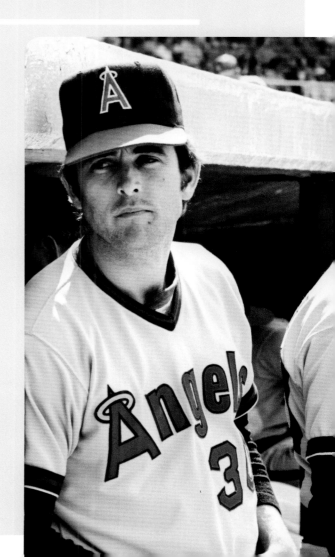

As Reggie Jackson said, "Every hitter likes fastballs just like everybody likes ice cream. But you don't like it when someone's stuffing it into you by the gallon. That's how you feel when Ryan's throwing balls by you."

Below Ryan was as popular with fans as he was intimidating to hitters.

Above Ryan and teammate Ellie Rodriguez commemorate the four no-hitters Ryan pitched for the Angels.

1966–1993

NOLAN RYAN BY THE (AMAZING) NUMBERS

Major League Baseball

★★★

The most dominating pitcher of his generation, Nolan Ryan was a nearly unhittable strikeout machine. During his 27-year Hall of Fame career, he put up numbers that may never be matched.

Seven no-hitters. Most in the history of baseball. Four of them for the Angels: two in 1973 and one each in both 1974 and 1975.

5,714 career strikeouts. Most in the history of base-ball. He struck out 2,416 as an Angel.

Led the American League in strikeouts seven of the eight years he pitched for the Angels and had his five highest single-season totals with the club.

Completed 20 or more games five times with the Angels.

Made eight All-Star teams, five with the Angels.

Won 324 career games, 138 with the Angels.

383 strikeouts in 1973. Most in the modern (post-1900) history of baseball. He also is No. 4, No. 8, No. 10, and No. 12 on the all-time single-season strikeout list. All five of those seasons were with the Angels.

He struck out 19 batters in a game three times, all with the Angels.

Above The indomitable Nolan Ryan, leader of the Angels pitching staff during the 1970s.

Bobby Winkles, who managed Ryan in '74, said, "Nolan was indestructible. He had the best work habits of any player I've ever seen in baseball. If you went out to the mound to remove him, he'd just say, 'Who would you rather have pitching to the next guy, me or the fella warming up in the bullpen?' So, I'd leave him in."

The decade evolved from strong pitching, led by the indomitable Ryan, to a power team that would win the first championship in team history.

But it was the pitchers who dominated the early '70s. Besides Ryan, who would eventually be elected to baseball's Hall of Fame by 98.8 percent of the vote in 1999, there was Clyde Wright, Andy Messersmith, Bill Singer, and Frank Tanana.

Wright, who would accurately be described as a cunning lefty, won 22 games, became an All-Star, and threw a no-hitter in 1970.

It was July 3 at Anaheim Stadium, and Wright had been inducted into the NAIA Baseball Hall of Fame prior to a game he was scheduled to pitch against Oakland. After Skeeter had warmed up, pitching coach Norm Sherry told him to "pitch a no-hitter so you can get in another Hall of Fame tonight." Wright did just that, fashioning the first no-no in the stadium's history. Wright, who was making $18,000 that year, was rewarded with a $500 bonus from Gene Autry. "I bought everyone one drink, and [catcher] Joe Azcue as many as he wanted," laughed Wright, who admitted afterward that he was nervous. "After the seventh inning, I went down into the runway, and I sat there shaking, trying not to think about it," he told Dave Distel of the *Los Angeles Times*.

Wright had won just one game in 1969, and, when asked the difference between '69 and '70, he always answered "21." He was named the American League Comeback Player of the Year.

Wright, who was making $18,000 that year, was rewarded with a $500 bonus from Gene Autry. "I bought everyone one drink and [catcher] Joe Azcue as many as he wanted," laughed Wright.

Above Clyde Wright posted a 2.83 ERA in his big 1970 season.

JULY 3, 1970
CLYDE WRIGHT'S NO-HITTER

The "Big A"

Clyde Wright was the American League Comeback Player of the Year in 1970, increasing his win total from 1 game in 1969 to 22 in 1970. The highlight of his season came on a Friday night before a small crowd of just over 12,000 at Anaheim Stadium, known affectionately as the "Big A."

Wright pitched the first no-hitter in the stadium, defeating the Oakland A's, 4–0. He walked four, and his only strikeout victim was Reggie Jackson, who took a called third strike in the fourth inning. He induced 14 ground ball outs, including a double play off the bat of Felipe Alou to end the game.

Roger Repoz tripled and scored in the first inning to give Wright the only run he would need, while third baseman Ken McMullen hit a three-run home run in the fourth to pad the lead.

Q&A with CLYDE WRIGHT

ON HIS NO-HITTER . . .

It was just another time to go out and warm up. But there's a funny story about that night. I went to a small college in Tennessee, and that night they inducted me into the NAIA Hall of Fame. Norm Sherry, my pitching coach, was there, and when I came in the dugout after the ceremony he said, "Why don't you go out and throw a no-hitter? That'll get you in the other Hall of Fame." I still wasn't thinking about it, but I went out and threw a no-hitter. Joe Azcue, my catcher, called a perfect game. Every time he put down a finger, that was it. I think I only shook him off twice out of 98 pitches.

ON GETTING CALLED UP TO THE MAJOR LEAGUES . . .

I was with our AA team playing a game in Arkansas, and my phone rang. Ballplayers always play tricks on each other, prank phone calls and all that. That time, when my phone rang, the guy on the other end said, "This is Fred Haney, the general manager of the Angels."

I said, "Sure it is, Fred," and then I hung up the phone.

A couple of minutes later, my phone range again. The same voice came over the wire and said, "Can you play with the big boys?"

I said to myself, "Oh my goodness, it *is* Fred Haney."

So that day, I flew out and joined the big league ball club.

ON HIS FIRST DAYS WITH THE ANGELS . . .

There was not much culture shock for me. It didn't really bother me, because all I came out here for was to play baseball. I spent most of my time at the baseball stadium. We would all get to the stadium before noon and sit in the clubhouse and talk about this and that and play cards.

ON DEAN CHANCE . . .

He was tough. Catching one of his throws was like catching a piece of concrete in your hand. He had more natural ability to throw a fastball. He would turn his back to you if you were a hitter, and you didn't know whether it was going low or away or up or in. You couldn't see it until right at the last split second.

ON JIM FREGOSI . . .

Jim Fregosi had the talent, but he was not a born superstar. He made himself into one of the best short-stops in the league because of the way he played. He played hard, and he played every day. He even played hurt.

ON BUCK RODGERS . . .

Buck was just super. I loved to pitch to him. It didn't matter what day it was or who I was pitching against. We just always had a good time playing.

Andy Messersmith, a local product from nearby Western High School in Anaheim, won 20 the following season, and Bill Singer, acquired in one of the biggest trades in franchise history, joined Ryan as a 20-game winner in '73. Singer, Frank Robinson, Bobby Valentine, Billy Grabarkewitz, and Mike Strahler had been acquired from the Dodgers for Messersmith and Ken McMullen over the previous winter. Singer and Ryan combined for 624 strikeouts that season, a modern-day record for two pitchers on the same staff.

Tanana, a self-assured, smooth-throwing lefty from Detroit, joined the rotation at age 20 in 1974. He, too, had a blazing fastball and superior control. From '75 to '78, he won 82 games and recorded 81 complete games, including 14 in a row at one point in '77. He led the league in strikeouts once, led in ERA during the '75 season, and fanned 17 in one unforgettable game. Tanana appeared headed for a Ryanesque career, but an arm injury derailed him by the end of the decade.

The Fregosi-Ryan trade and the blockbuster seven-player deal with the Dodgers in '72 were not the only significant player moves of the decade.

Right Bill Singer, the former Dodger, worked well with Nolan Ryan—the two combined for 624 strikeouts during the 1973 season.

Above Nolan Ryan, the Angels' ace.

Left Left-hander Frank Tanana threw 14 consecutive complete games in 1977.

The Angels had a new outfielder in 1970, courtesy of a trade with Cincinnati (that included pitcher Jim McGlothlin going to the Reds). His name was Alex Johnson, and he could hit. In his first season in Anaheim, Johnson hit .329 and won the AL batting championship, the only Angel to ever do so. But he was moody and difficult, and his career was short-lived. Johnson was the first of a number of skilled hitters who made their way to Anaheim in the '70s for brief stops.

Tony Conigliaro was another star-crossed figure. A Red Sox favorite, he came to the Angels in '71 after a terrific comeback season in Boston (36 homers, 116 RBI). He was hitting only .222 on July 9 when he called an early-morning press conference to announce his retirement (after striking out six times and going hitless in eight at bats in a 20-inning loss to the A's in Oakland the night before).

Above (clockwise from top left) Former Dodgers John Roseboro, Bill Singer, Don Drysdale, Frank Robinson, Jeff Torborg, Bill Grabarkewitz, Ron Perranoski, and Bobby Valentine joined the Halos before the 1973 season.

Left Alex Johnson posted a .329 average to claim the batting title in 1970.

Q&A with FRANK TANANA

ON THE DAY HE STRUCK OUT 17 BATTERS, JUNE 21, 1975 . . .

I loved strikeouts, and that day I just kept striking people out. It was a funny thing that day: Either they got a hit (I think I gave up nine hits), or they struck out. It was also pretty cool to think I did not walk anybody that game, that I had great control. I got those 17 strikeouts in eight innings, and I did not get a strikeout in the ninth. I wanted it bad and tried very hard to strike someone out because I knew I had a good number going.

ON ROD CAREW . . .

You knew Rod Carew had to be good because he was the greatest hitter of our era. I admired the way he played the game and the way he could swing the bat. His ability was beyond question. It was just very nice and a lot of fun to always get to be a teammate of someone that you've only seen from afar. Rodney was a nice man; he was just a wonderful teammate.

OCTOBER 1, 1970

ALEX JOHNSON WINS AL BATTING TITLE

The "Big A"

Alex Johnson singled in his last two times at bat to win the American League batting championship with a .329 average, edging Boston's Carl Yastrzemski by .0003 (.3289 to .3286).

It was the first—and remains the only—time an Angel has won the batting championship.

Following two seasons in which he hit over .300, Johnson was acquired by the Angels—along with infielder Chico Ruiz—from the Cincinnati Reds for

former All-Star pitcher Jim McGlothlin, Pedro Borbon, and Vern Geishert.

An enigmatic performer who had both power and speed (he stole 17 of 19 bases that season), Johnson was often criticized by fans and media for his lack of hustle and passion.

He was traded to the Cleveland Indians for Vada Pinson following the 1971 season.

Another slugger in the Angels lineup during the '70s was Frank Robinson, one of the more compelling figures ever to play under the Halo. A two-time Most Valuable Player, Robinson was, at 37, near the end of a brilliant Hall of Fame career. He arrived in Anaheim after an average season with the Dodgers. But he was not yet done. He homered his first time up for the Angels and hit 30 for the season with 97 RBI. As fiery a competitor who ever played the game, Robinson was given a chance to manage the Cleveland Indians the following year, so the Angels traded him, allowing Robinson to become the first African American manager in the major leagues.

Then there was Bobby Bonds, who displayed his unique combination of power and speed by hitting 37 home runs, driving in 115 runs, and stealing 41 bases in '77.

The most tragic story of the decade was that of Lyman Bostock, an unusually gifted hitter, who came to the Angels for the 1978 season. After a slow start in which he offered to return his salary, the career .300 hitter had his average back up to .296 after a day game in Chicago. But that night, he was murdered in his hometown of nearby Gary, Indiana, shot to death by the ex-husband of a woman Bostock had just met. He was 28 years old.

Not everyone had short stays under the Big A. Brian Downing, who attended nearby Magnolia High School and Cypress College, and who did not play baseball before his brief experience on the college team, was acquired in a 1978 trade with the White Sox (for Bonds). He had an undistinguished career in Chicago and didn't do much in '78, his first season with the Angels, hitting a soft .255. But that off-season, he undertook a rigorous weight-training program and altered his batting stance to a wide-open one. The results were staggering, and Downing became a prolific hitter in the Angels batting order for the next dozen years. In '79 he hit .326, third best in the American League. When he finished his career with the Angels in 1990, he held team records for games played, at bats, hits, runs, doubles, home runs, and runs batted in. Downing was a rock-solid performer in the middle of the ever-changing Angels offense.

Above Brian Downing joined the Angels in 1978 and played with the team until 1990.

Right Gene Autry welcomes Lyman Bostock to the Angels in 1978.

APRIL 6, 1973
FRANK ROBINSON'S DEBUT

The "Big A"

With President Richard Nixon among the 27,240 fans on hand for the season opener, 37-year-old slugger Frank Robinson hit the first pitch thrown to him for a home run over the left field wall, and the Angels were victorious, 3–2, over the Kansas City Royals.

Robinson had had only seven at bats during limited Spring Training because of a leg injury but hit his 523rd career homer off Steve Busby leading off the second inning.

Robinson, acquired from the Dodgers in a big multiplayer deal in the off-season, also threw a runner out at third base.

Nolan Ryan struck out 12 Royals and went the distance for the win.

Nolan Ryan's Angels debut in 1972 coincided with the arrival of another important Angel, one who never pitched, hit, fielded, or managed. Jimmie Reese had already had a long and memorable career in baseball when the Angels hired him to be their conditioning coach . . . at age 71. Reese began his life in baseball back in 1919 as a batboy with the Pacific Coast League Angels. He played most of his career in the PCL, although he spent two seasons with the New York Yankees (1930 and '31), where he roomed with Babe Ruth and famously said, "I roomed with Babe's suitcase." During the next 22 seasons with the Angels, Reese was known for his ability to hit fungos with his own specially designed bat. He was a gentle and beloved man. Ryan even named one of his children after him.

After the stability of Bill Rigney's tenure as the Angels manager in the '60s, the '70s proved more turbulent as the team employed seven different managers—Lefty Phillips, Del Rice, Bobby Winkles (who had won three national championships on the collegiate level at Arizona State), Dick Williams (a future Hall of Famer), Norm Sherry, Dave Garcia, and Jim Fregosi.

And despite their outstanding pitching in the early part of the decade, the Angels were a second-division team, never finishing higher than third in the six-team American League West from 1970 to 1977.

But with the advent of free agency, the Angels opened their wallets and began bringing some prominent players to Anaheim. Don Baylor, Bobby Grich, and Joe Rudi were signed in 1977, and Rod Carew, a seven-time batting champion who was on the verge of free agency, came in a trade with Minnesota in '79.

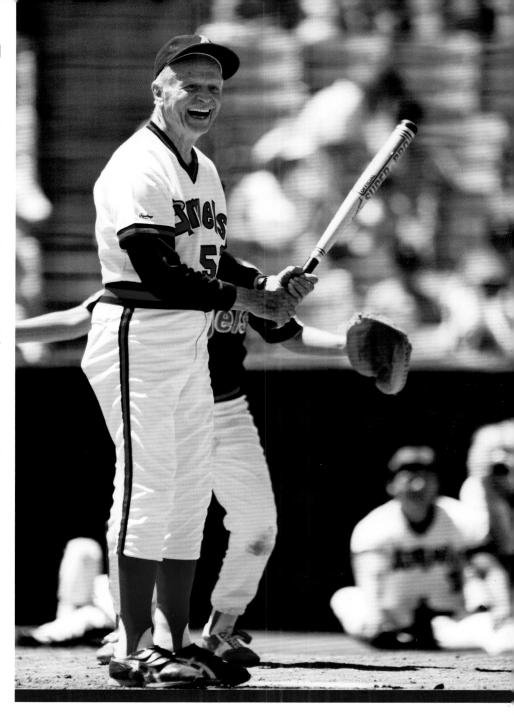

Top Right Jimmie Reese made the fungo famous.

Right Reese loved to share his knowledge of the game.

Reese began his life in baseball back in 1919 as a batboy with the Pacific Coast League Angels. He played most of his career in the PCL, although he spent two seasons with the New York Yankees (1930 and '31), where he roomed with Babe Ruth and famously said, "I roomed with Babe's suitcase."

Above Manager Jim Fregosi and Gene Autry
welcome veteran Rod Carew to the Angels.

"Watching Carew hit is like watching Bulova make a watch, De Beers cut a diamond, Stradivarius varnish a violin, or Michelangelo do a ceiling," wrote Murray.

Carew, according to the *Los Angeles Times'* legendary Jim Murray, made hitting an art form: "Watching Carew hit is like watching Bulova make a watch, De Beers cut a diamond, Stradivarius varnish a violin, or Michelangelo do a ceiling," wrote Murray.

Grich (52 games) and Rudi (64 games) were unable to help much in that first year due to injuries. Baylor did make a big contribution, though, with 25 home runs.

Harry Dalton, who had a reputation of never seeing a trade he didn't like, was at the helm as general manager in the mid-'70s.

Other pieces were beginning to come together. In '75, the Angels drafted Carney Lansford out of Santa Clara. Following his big '77 season, Bonds was traded to the Chicago White Sox in a deal that would yield pitchers Dave Frost and Chris Knapp along with Brian Downing. Another trade brought Dan Ford from Minnesota in '78.

In the middle of the '78 season, Dave Garcia was relieved of his managerial duties, and the Angels brought back their prodigal son, Fregosi, to run the team. The team climbed to second place under Fregosi's leadership.

In 1979, the Angels finally got to the top of the baseball mountain. The club was in first place for 134 days during the season and clinched its first American League West Championship on September 25. Baylor was the Most Valuable Player in the league, hitting 36 home runs and driving in 139. Grich chimed in with 30 home runs and 101 RBI, and Ford added 21 and 101. Downing hit .326, and Carew .318. The Angels scored 866 runs, a club record that would remain until the team scored 883 in 2009.

"That team had the best chemistry of any team I've ever played on," said Grich. "And it was the most fun I had in my 17-year career. The catalyst was Rod Carew. When we got him from Minnesota, we got not only an All-Star and a Hall of Famer in our locker room but someone who drew a lot of the attention from the media and gave the rest of us a chance to relax and play baseball."

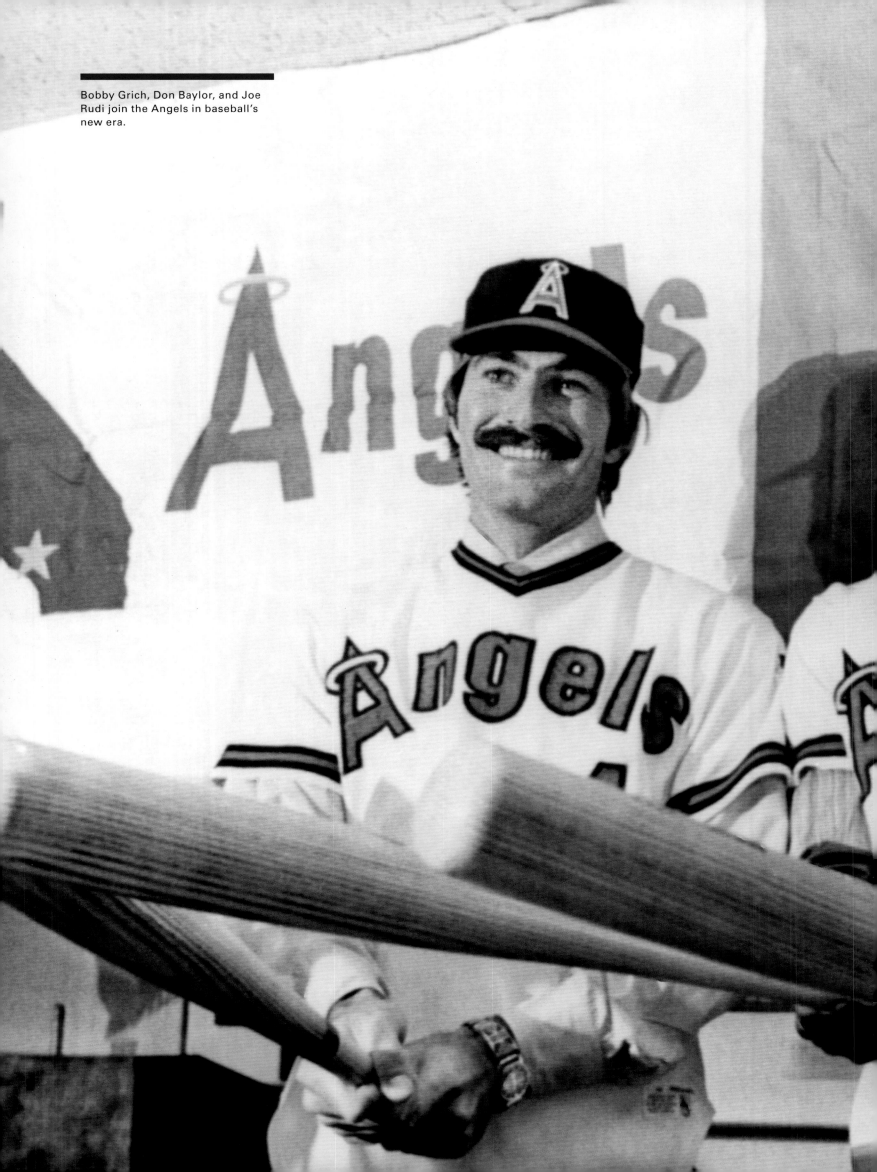

Bobby Grich, Don Baylor, and Joe Rudi join the Angels in baseball's new era.

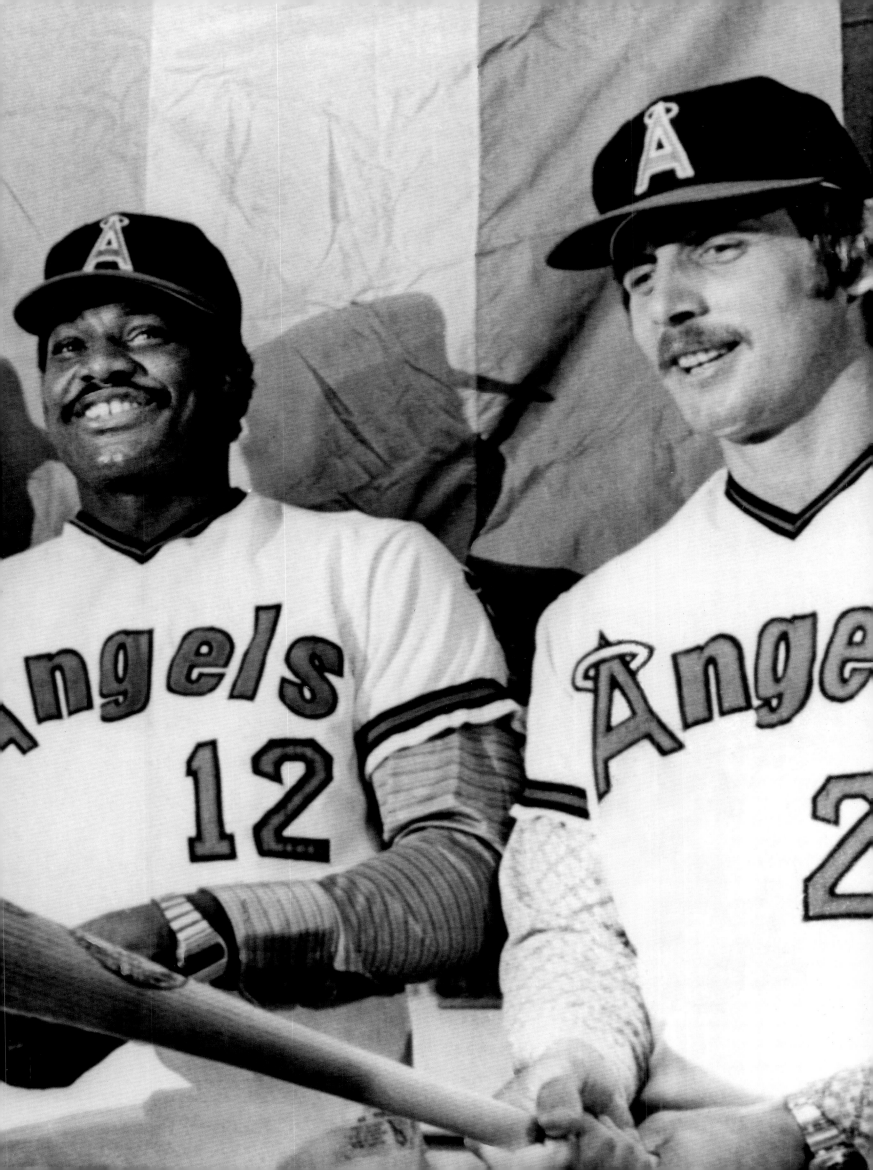

ON JOINING THE ANGELS . . .

Nolan Ryan and Frank Tanana were playing for the Angels. Then the team started to bring in some offensive players. I signed first, Joe Rudi signed the following day, and Grich joined a couple of days later. Everybody wanted to come to Southern California and play for the Angels. I could see that I was going to hit in a lineup with Grich and Rudi, and that really helped out.

ON MANAGER JIM FREGOSI . . .

When Fregosi came here, he wanted to make sure that the Angels were on the map. He was for the Angels, heart and soul. There is no doubt that he was the leader of our club, and we played the way he wanted us to play. It was so much fun when we rolled into 1979 with renewed confidence.

ON NOLAN RYAN . . .

Nolan Ryan had the best fastball and the best curveball. He always gave us an edge, and the opposition had to bear down to play against him. He was one of the greatest teammates, and he was also a great intimidator.

ON THE DIVISION CHAMPIONSHIP IN 1979 . . .

It was a crazy celebration on the field and in the clubhouse. I have a picture of Mr. Autry and President Nixon cheering with us in the clubhouse. I remember thinking, "We finally made it." There was finally that national recognition—the Angels finally, finally made it. It was quite a feeling, and I know every player in that clubhouse sensed it.

ON ROD CAREW . . .

Carew was off the charts. He would be ready to go before Spring Training even started. Five days into Spring Training, I think he would get bored because he was already ready. He was an incredible guy to have as a teammate. He was the best bunter in the game. The other team would move in on him and keep moving in, but still they could not throw him out. He could get a base hit any day of the week, on Christmas or Thanksgiving. That's just the way it was with Rod.

ON JIMMIE REESE . . .

He was a true gentleman who would not say anything bad about anybody. He roomed with Babe Ruth, though he said he roomed with the Babe's suitcases. He would frame pictures for us. He was just a wealth of baseball information.

1979 DON BAYLOR'S MVP SEASON

★★★

A 139-RBI season helped earn Don Baylor the Most Valuable Player Award in the American League in 1979, the first Angel to win the award.

The big year by the 30-year-old Baylor catapulted the Angels to their first division title with an 88-74 record.

For the season, Baylor hit .296 with 36 home runs and led the league in both RBI and runs scored, with 120. He was the runaway winner of the MVP Award, receiving 20 of 28 first-place votes, with no other player receiving more than 3.

Baylor, the Angels' designated hitter in '79, got off to a blazing start, driving in a then league-record 28 runs in April, and never cooled off. On April 21, he belted a grand slam during the Angels 13–1 victory over the A's. On May 15, Baylor beat the Brewers with a leadoff home run in the bottom of the ninth to break a 1–1 tie.

On August 8, Baylor was already sitting at 98 RBI and hit the century mark in style, connecting in the third inning off the A's Matt Keough for a two-run shot for Nos. 99 and 100. Baylor went 4 for 5 with that home run and later added an RBI single for No. 101.

But the man they called Groove was hardly satisfied with that. On August 25, Baylor had one of the best single days in Angels history against Toronto, as the Angels blistered the Blue Jays, 24–2. Baylor belted two home runs and drove in a career-high eight runs.

"I chose the Angels, in part, because former teammates Lyman Bostock and Dan Ford told me what a great guy Gene [Autry] was and that they were close to winning," said Carew. "And '79 was an exciting year; everyone contributed."

It was a Tuesday. September 25, 1979. Frank Tanana pitching for the Angels against Kansas City. A near-capacity crowd of 40,631 were rocking and rolling with YES WE CAN signs and chants.

Downing ripped a pair of run-scoring singles, and Tanana pitched a nifty five-hitter in the clincher, 4–1.

"It felt like the whole stadium was closing in on us after the last out," said Carew. "People were climbing over the railings and racing onto the field."

AUTRY FINALLY HAS ANOTHER CHAMPION, read the *Los Angeles Times* headline the next day, a reference to the Angels owner and his longtime companion, the golden palomino Champion. Autry's guest that night, Richard Nixon, saw the team end 19 years of frustration by winning a division title for the first time. Infielder Jim Anderson even poured some Champagne on the former president. In the postgame celebration, Ryan said of Autry, "I imagine he's about as happy right now as he can remember being."

Fregosi wore a lucky T-shirt under his uniform jersey on the historic clinching night. The words printed on it: YES, WE DID. ANGELS. 1979 WESTERN DIVISION CHAMPIONSHIP.

Left A clubhouse leader in his playing days, Jim Fregosi took the helm and led the Angels as manager from 1978 to 1981.

"That team had the best chemistry of any team I've ever played on," said Grich. "And it was the most fun I had in my 17-year career."

Left Rod Carew meets President Richard Nixon as Gene Autry looks on.

Q&A with BRIAN DOWNING

ON BREAKING INTO THE MAJOR LEAGUES . . .

I really did lousy in high school. I went to junior college to try to play some more, and I sat on the bench the entire season, on a team that won two games the whole year. When that season ended, I signed a professional contract. The only reason I signed is, growing up, I knew a scout who said if there was ever any way to sign me, he would find it, and he did. I had a lot of versatility, and he said, "This guy can play every position, and he can run, he can throw—you can sign him for nothing." And that's how I got in the door.

ON HIS TRAINING REGIMEN . . .

I made the conversion to go to free weights, and that is really what turned me around. I played at home a lot and erected a batting cage in my backyard. Being able to work out there for hours and hours every day before I went to the stadium really got me going in the right direction.

ON THE 1979 SEASON . . .

That was our first success as an organization, so the whole season was magical. We had great efforts from a lot of people: Bobby Grich had a great year; Don Baylor took the MVP. There was just a whole lot going on with the "Yes We Can" year. Just a tremendous year. The first time you win is really special.

ON MOVING FROM CATCHER TO OUTFIELDER . . .

I had nothing to do with it. One day, I came to the park, and I had a seven behind my name on the lineup card. I came there ready to catch, and when I saw the seven, I thought, "Uh-oh." It was something I had never done before, and to do it in a big league park . . . I was scared to death. But I knew physically that I had to be out there.

ON GENE MAUCH . . .

I really had a kinship with Gene Mauch. We just had something between us. I would be at the plate, and I would just look at him, and he would know what I wanted to do. We did not need signs to communicate in those situations

ON MANAGER JIM FREGOSI . . .

He was an "everyday player" guy as a manager. Everyday players just gravitated to him. I liked how he needled the guys that could take it. He did that to me, and it pushed me. But I like aggressive people, and I guess that is why I liked him as manager.

"It felt like the whole stadium was closing in on us after the last out," said Carew. "People were climbing over the railings and racing onto the field."

The Angels traveled to Baltimore for their first playoff games. They had not fared well during the regular season (3-9) to an Oriole team that sported a Hall of Fame manager in the dugout, Earl Weaver; a Hall of Fame first baseman, Eddie Murray; and the Cy Young Award winner at the front of the rotation, Mike Flanagan (a 23-game winner that season). The Orioles had won 102 games that year and won the first 2 against the Angels in Baltimore.

The Angels avoided a sweep and got their initial playoff win on October 5 in Anaheim. Baylor homered in the first inning, but it was an Oriole error by center fielder Al Bumbry and a pinch-hit double by seldom-used Larry Harlow that produced two runs and the win in the bottom of the ninth, 4–3. Baltimore closed it out the following day, 8–0. Carew hit .412 in the series, and Ford had two homers, both in Baltimore.

Q&A with DICK ENBERG

ON NOLAN RYAN . . .

Nolan Ryan always had the potential of throwing a no-hitter. He did it enough times that fans started to look ahead and say, "Ryan's pitching on Friday night, so let's get tickets for Friday, because he could throw another no-hitter."

His curveball snapped so sharply, it was impossible to hit. Hitters had to be ready for his fastball, and then he would throw the curve and it buckled their knees. Of all the people that I've met in more than 50 years of sports broadcasting, Nolan Ryan is one of the top ten greatest athletes—greatest people—that I've ever encountered.

ON FRANK TANANA . . .

He had great stuff. He was a left-hander that was so electric he could pitch inside to right–handers, and that was really the measuring stick: Are you good enough to throw a ball inside to a right-handed hitter? If you did not have good stuff and you threw inside to a right-handed hitter, that ball was over the fence. But Tanana had the kind of stuff that right-handers could not hit. He was quick–witted, and he was so clever in how he pitched.

ON HIS FIRST ANGELS BROADCAST . . .

My very first Angels play-by-play broadcast in 1969 was also my very first major league broadcast. I was so nervous, thinking, "This is it now. I'm a big league announcer."

Mr. Fred Haney, the general manager at the time, came into the booth and said, "I just want to come in and wish you luck and give you one piece of advice: Report the ball. Don't tell me what you hope it does or what you think it's going to do. Just report the ball."

It was great advice, because whenever I was in trouble and the ball was not doing anything, I would go back and say, "The ball is in his hand. The pitcher is rubbing up the ball. He backs up. He hides the ball behind his back." And that always got me back into the flow of the game.

ON THE ANGELS 2002 WORLD SERIES VICTORY . . .

I was flying home during the seventh game of the World Series, and I asked the flight attendant if the pilot could find out the score, and if he did would he please announce it. A few minutes later the pilot came on the PA and said, "The Angels have won the World Series," and I started to cry tears of joy. It was the culmination of all those years, and I was so happy for all the people who had lived through the growth and birth of this team, and now we had finally won.

SEPTEMBER 25, 1979

AUTRY HAS ANOTHER CHAMPION

The "Big A"

★★★

The Angels managed no extra base hits, only singles—but a dozen of them—to defeat Kansas City, 4–1, to win the American League West for the first time.

Leadoff hitter Rick Miller, Rod Carew (batting in the unaccustomed fifth spot in the order), and Brian Downing each collected three singles.

Downing drove in the first run of the game in the second, Carew scored on a wild pitch, and Larry Harlow drove in Downing, who had another RBI single, in the fifth after Kansas City had scored its only run of the game against Frank Tanana, who went the distance and pitched a five-hitter.

Angels fans Bill Kristinat and Paul Walker were credited with the "Yes We Can" slogan that followed the Angels all season long at home and that became "Yes We Did" after the clincher against Kansas City. Kristinat and Walker were rewarded by throwing out the first pitch on opening day in 1980.

Angels attendance increased by 50 percent in 1979.

Wrote the *Los Angeles Times'* Jim Murray, "For the 19th straight year, there will be no lovable, old character in cowboy boots and a 10-gallon hat leading his team into the World Series."

Attendance had risen dramatically in the '70s. From '70 to '76, the team averaged 941,000 fans per season. In '77, the mark was 1.4 million; the next year, 1.7 million; and in the '79 championship season, 2.5 million, ranking second in the American League.

Both Ryan's No. 30 and Reese's No. 50 have been retired by the Angels.

Wrote the *Los Angeles Times'* Jim Murray, "For the 19th straight year, there will be no lovable, old character in cowboy boots and a 10-gallon hat leading his team into the World Series."

Left Nolan Ryan's pitching helped bring fans to the ballpark and contributed to the Angels' increased popularity during the 1970s.

CHAPTER 3: 1980s

MAUCH
AND
MEMORIES

Slugger Reggie Jackson
acknowledges the fans'
salute.

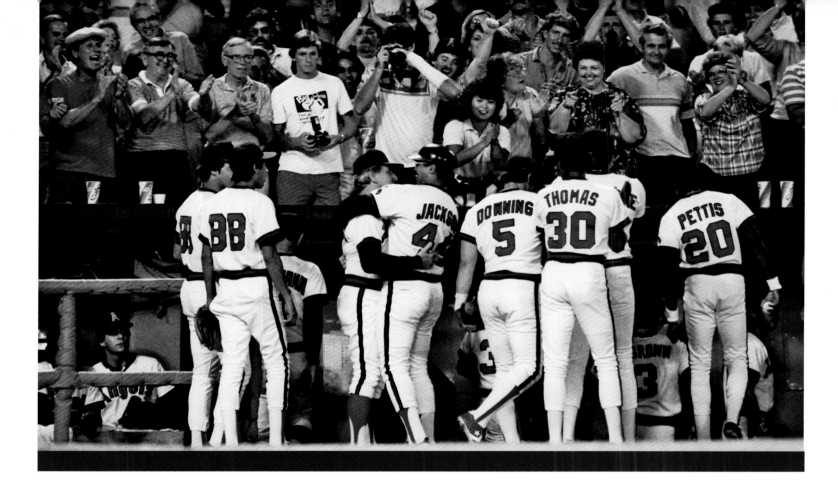

The 1980s were a decade of near misses and milestones, of glory and heartbreak. Of the Little General, Mr. October, and a player who had his own world.

Gene Mauch, "the Little General," led the team to division titles in both '82 and '86, only to lose two wrenching playoff series. Reggie Jackson, who had become Mr. October for his recent World Series heroics, Rod Carew, and Don Sutton all reached significant statistical achievements in their Hall of Fame careers, and Anaheim Stadium became Wally World when a rookie first baseman from BYU, Wally Joyner, exploded on the scene in 1986.

Attendance sizzled at the Big A. The Angels drew more than 2.2 million fans every year except the strike-shortened '81 season. They ranked first in attendance in the league four times and second twice—all in a six-year span.

The Stadium was packed for several reasons: The Angels fielded good teams and exciting ones, and there were plenty of stars in the home-team dugout. The Los Angeles Rams of the NFL moved in as cotenants at Anaheim in 1980, and the stadium was expanded to a capacity of over 64,000.

Jim Fregosi had been replaced in mid-1981 after a second-division '80 season and a slow start the following year. Enter Mauch.

Gene William Mauch was born to baseball. He had played the game on the sandlots of Los Angeles, had been an infielder in both the majors and minors, and began managing at the age of 27 in the Southern Association. He had already logged 21 years as a major league manager with the Phillies, Expos, and Twins before being hired in 1981 in Anaheim.

Top Angels fans turned out in record numbers to watch the teams of the 1980s, more than 2.2 million each season.

Above Gene Mauch knew baseball's best strategies inside and out.

Jackson then went on to say the Angels "should win 88 to 90 games" (they would win 93) and "I do think the Angels wanted me because they felt I'd bring a certain ingredient to the club, something beyond driving the bus that brings the fans to the park."

Known for his love of small ball, Mauch emphasized defense, speed, and fundamentals. He favored the bunt, sacrifice, and hit-and-run. "He's a complicated man," wrote Jim Murray in the *Los Angeles Times*. "He's as intense as a light bulb, as explosive as six sticks of dynamite in a bouncing truck."

Then there was Reginald Martinez "Reggie" Jackson, the self-proclaimed "straw that stirs the drink," who had been lured to Anaheim with a large free-agent contract after his years as Mr. October in New York. At his January 26 press conference at the stadium, Carew, Don Baylor, Fred Lynn, and Rick Burleson serenaded Jackson with chants of "Reg-gie, Reg-gie, Reg-gie!" to make the former Yankee feel at home. Jackson then went on to say the Angels "should win 88 to 90 games" (they would win 93) and "I do think the Angels wanted me because they felt I'd bring a certain ingredient to the club, something beyond driving the bus that brings the fans to the park.

"I'd hate to think they got me just to help attendance, though I can see the Angels drawing 3 million and I'm confident they'll make money off me." The club drew 2.8 million, their highest total in history to that point, and Jackson did have a clause that paid him additional monies based on attendance, 50 cents for every patron over 2.4 million.

Reggie, of course, was news. In March of that year, he graced the cover of *Sports Illustrated* in his new Angels uniform under the headline HARK THE HERALDED ANGEL SWINGS."

The '82 team had a bonanza of star power. All eight offensive regulars had been All-Stars (Carew, Bobby Grich, Burleson, Doug DeCinces, Brian Downing, Lynn, Baylor, and Jackson), and four of them had been MVPs of the league (Jackson, Carew, Baylor, and Lynn). Despite Mauch's preference for playing the game from base to base, his team could launch plenty of long balls, too, especially Jackson, who tied for the league lead in home runs with 39. All told, five players hit 20 or more home runs and drove in 84 or more runs. (It was also the oldest team in club history, with an average age of 32.3 years.)

Two of the most exciting series ever in Anaheim took place that summer. The Angels, playing against the best of the American League, displayed big-game style and a flair for the dramatic against the Kansas City Royals and the New York Yankees. On June 26, before a Saturday crowd of 56,794, Baylor smashed a two-run home run in the bottom

of the 12th off KC's accomplished reliever, Dan Quisenberry for a 6–5 win. A day later, 36,592 were on hand to cheer as the Angels registered four more home runs (Baylor, Downing, DeCinces, and Juan Beniquez) for a 9–1 win.

On a steamy weekend in July, the Yankees came strutting into town and the Angels slapped them in striking fashion. On Friday night, July 9, more than 41,000 packed the Big A to see Geoff Zahn, a soft-tossing southpaw, throw a two-hitter at the Bronx Bombers. Again, it was Baylor with a homer in the 4–1 win. Over 53,000 came out the next day, and the Angels erupted for 10 runs in the third inning en route to a 12–6 laugher. Jackson homered twice, and Lynn added another. The Angels capped the three-game sweep with a 2–1 victory on Sunday when Downing delivered a home run off Goose Gossage in the eighth before 44,834 fans. The Angels drew 139,796 people over the weekend.

In a crucial midweek series against Kansas City in late September, the Angels swept the Royals to take a three-game lead in the West. They never looked back, and won their second division title in four years.

Above Jackson won the 1982 Silver Slugger award with 101 RBIs and 39 home runs.

Left Doug DeCinces and Brian Downing celebrate while Dick Schofield looks on.

Reggie Jackson always commanded attention, whether it came from the media, the fans, or the opposing pitcher.

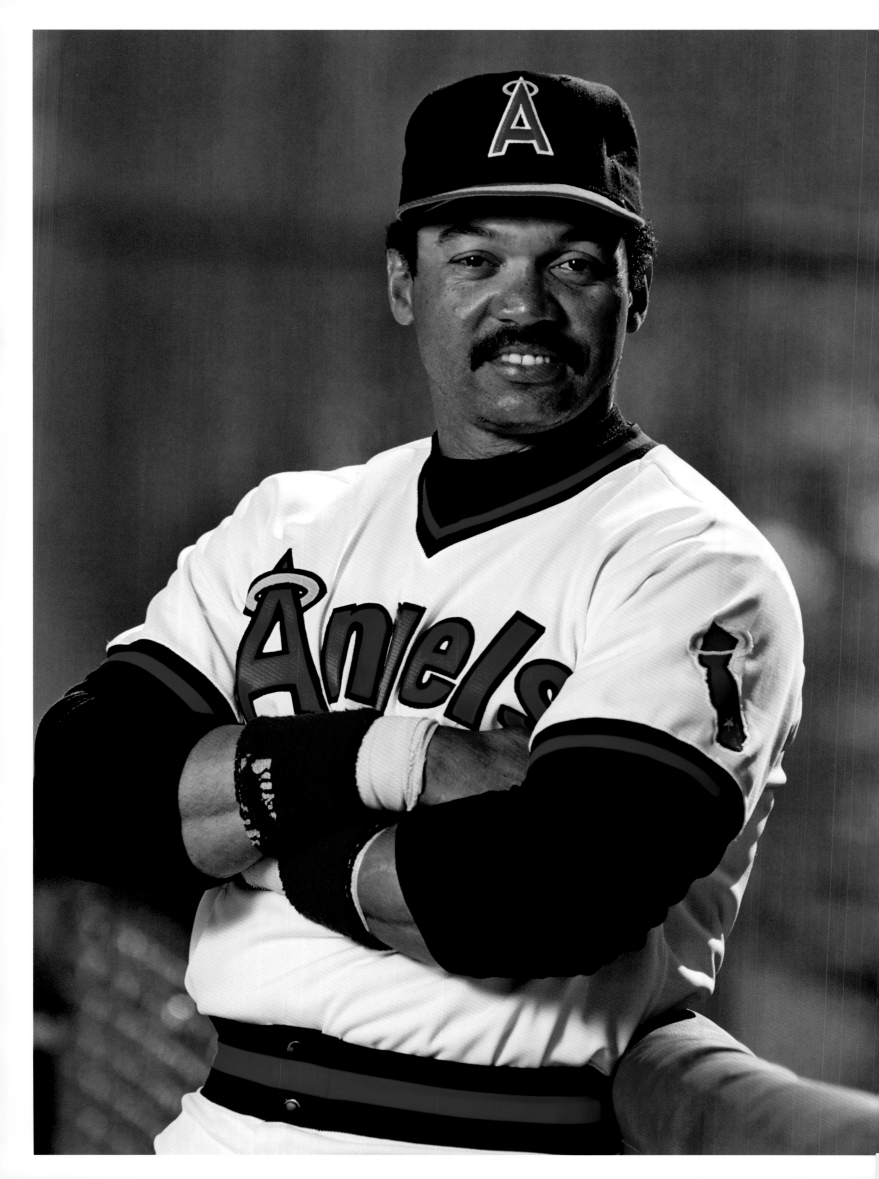

Q&A with REGGIE JACKSON

ON HIS TEAMMATES . . .

I really thought our clubhouse was solid. Bobby Grich did his thing. Doug DeCinces was a mature professional. Rod Carew could hit underground, in the dark. Freddy Lynn was an outstanding defender in center field. So we had a heck of a good ball club with a lot of talent.

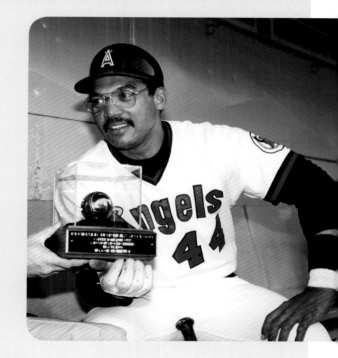

ON GENE MAUCH . . .

I enjoyed playing for Gene Mauch because he was prepared all the time. I went to the ballpark one time at six o'clock in the morning, and it was the first time I caught him out of uniform. He had his shirt on and he was sitting there in his underwear and street shoes. I never got to the ballpark before him, and I have nothing but positive things to say about him.

ON JIMMIE REESE . . .

Jimmie Reese, he could exercise you. He would run you back and forth across the field with a fungo. He could play catch with you with a fungo. They say he could throw batting practice with a fungo—I never saw him, but I wouldn't be surprised if he could have. Just before batting practice, he worked me out and got me loose by running me from side to side, back and forth, hitting me ground balls, and that was my way of getting worked out for 10 to 15 minutes before every game.

ON NOLAN RYAN . . .

When you played against Nolan on a Saturday afternoon or a Sunday afternoon, you were going to have the whole afternoon with him. The game would start at one o'clock, and at five o'clock he would be on the mound no matter the score. He was going to be on that mound all day, and you knew you were going to have an afternoon barbecue with Nolan Ryan.

ON BRIAN DOWNING . . .

He was a very quiet, strong person. Brian was always a family man. I appreciated his character and what he stood for as a person.

ON HIS 500TH HOME RUN . . .

On September 17, 1984, I hit my 500th home run in the same spot that I hit home run No. 1, in the same ballpark (the "Big A"), against Kansas City. I hit my first home run against the Angels there, and I hit No. 500 for the Angels there, and both home runs came off of left-handed pitchers. So it was just ironic.

Q&A with BOBBY GRICH

ON GROWING UP AN ANGELS FAN . . .

I was usually sitting about the fifth row, right in line with third base. Aurelio Rodriguez or Paul Schaal was the third baseman, and I was watching Fregosi, Knoop, Don Mincher, Bob Rodgers, Jose Cardenal, Albie Pearson . . . I had that lineup down. I loved the Angels, I loved Angel Stadium, and it was a dream and a goal of mine to play on that field someday, and to be able to play for the Angels was the crème de la crème.

ON DON BAYLOR . . .

Donnie Baylor was always the stalwart in our locker room. He was the quiet leader, and he did not have a big ego. It was not about him, it was about winning as a team, and that was the kind of player he was. He led by example, and any time guys stepped out of line, he would be the first to let them know. And if Donnie said something to you, you pretty much paid attention.

ON BRIAN DOWNING . . .

He pushed himself and he made himself into a fantastic ballplayer. He is a self-made ballplayer from ground zero. He barely made the junior college team, and then he went on to become a great major league ballplayer.

ON SPRING TRAINING AT PALM SPRINGS . . .

We played in a real intimate stadium. The fans were just a few feet away. It built a lot of camaraderie between the players and the fans. It was a wonderful time for your hardcore baseball fan to really come out and see their players, get to know them on a personal basis. They would rope off the outfield and have extra people inside the fence out there, and it was a kick.

ON THE 1982 ANGELS . . .

It was the most talent-laden team I have ever played on in my career. We had a great defense at all positions, we had guys at the top and the bottom of the order who could hurt you, we had a strong pitching staff, and we had a lot of experience, a lot of guys who knew how to play the game. It was just a fun team to play on. I could not wait to come to the ballpark, because somebody was going to make a spectacular play that night—I just knew it.

JUNE 26–27, JULY 9–11, 1982
SIX BIG WINS

The "Big A"

★★★

In front of large and loud Anaheim Stadium crowds, the Angels won six pivotal games in the summer of 1982. Here's what they were saying after the games:

June 26. Angels 11, Royals 10. Don Baylor delivered the game winner against Kansas City's All-Star reliever, Dan Quisenberry. "It's like facing one King Kong after another," said Quisenberry of the Angels lineup.

June 27. Angels 9, Royals 1. Manager Gene Mauch rested regulars Rod Carew, Reggie Jackson, Fred Lynn, Bob Boone, and Tim Foli but still won. "I thought we'd win today, otherwise I wouldn't have put that lineup out there. I rest those people when I want to so they'll be ready when I need them," said Mauch.

July 9. Angels 4, Yankees 1. Soft-tossing left-hander Geoff Zahn pitched a two-hitter. Said New York's Lou Piniella, "I can't hit [Zahn]. I'll go on

the record with that. You have to be so patient, it's unbelievable. If he'd been in the league when I first came up, I'd be either bald, gray, or half crazy by now. It's like being bitten by a stuffed panda."

July 10. Angels 12, Yankees 6. Jackson, the former Yankee, hit two home runs. That year he hit 20 home runs and 47 RBI en route to a season with 39 home runs and 101 RBI. Said the slugger, "The man [Yankee owner George Steinbrenner] said I was done, but you're not done when you've done what I've done this year."

July 11. Angels 2, Yankees 1. Brian Downing hit the game-winning home run in the eighth inning, and the fans demanded he take a curtain call, which the reluctant Downing did. "I'm not a demonstrative person," he said. "The only reason I did today was because the crowd was getting louder and louder and the game might never have ended if I hadn't."

Right Don Baylor, Fred Lynn, and Rod Carew, three of the four MVPs who played for the Angels during the '80s. (Reggie Jackson was the fourth.)

Said Bobby Grich, "It was the most talented team I played on. We were a little underrated defensively, but the guys on the left side, Tim Foli [shortstop, who had replaced the injured Burleson] and DeCinces [third base] had outstanding defensive years. I played in Baltimore with Mark Belanger at short and Brooks Robinson at third, and in '82 Foli and DeCinces were every bit as good as those guys. And we were a smart team, too. Everyone knew how to play the game. I couldn't wait to get to the ballpark every night. It was fun. It was exciting."

The Angels had the playoff home-field advantage, thanks to a 93-69 regular-season record (the first time the franchise had ever won 90 games in a season), against the Milwaukee Brewers. Managed by Harvey Kuenn, the Brewers were long-ball hitters, cleverly nicknamed Harvey's Wallbangers.

In the first two games in Anaheim, the team played flawless ball with stout pitching, reliable fielding, and plenty of offense. They got a complete-game seven-hitter from Tommy John in the opening game, an 8–3 win, with Baylor driving home five runs and Lynn collecting three hits, including a home run. For the opener, the Angels drew their largest crowd in the history of the franchise, 64,406.

Bruce Kison followed John with another complete game, this one a five-hitter, and Jackson, in his element in October, hit a mammoth home run in a 4–2 victory.

The club needed but one win in Milwaukee to advance to the World Series for the first time. The Brewers, though, won Games 3 and 4, and the Angels fell one run short in Game 5, stranding the tying run on second base in the ninth inning in a heartbreaking 4–3 loss.

"I would like to have won it for Gene and Gene," said Jackson of Autry and Mauch, neither of whom would ever get to a World Series.

Lynn had, perhaps, his finest moment in an Angels uniform, winning MVP honors in a losing cause when he hit .611 in the five-game series.

An aging Angels team in '83—eight regulars were 31 or older—finished 70-92 under John McNamara, who had replaced Mauch. Baylor was gone to New York via free agency, while both Jackson and Lynn missed significant time with injuries.

Lynn, the former USC star, however, had a moment to remember. In Chicago in early July, the Angels center fielder became the first player in history to hit a grand slam home run in the All-Star game when he connected in the third inning to lead the American League to a resounding 13–3 win.

The Angels had added another local player to their stable when Mike Witt from Anaheim's Servite High School was drafted in 1978 and joined the rotation two years later. He would anchor the Angels rotation the entire decade and finish with 109 career wins. He blossomed in '84, winning

》》

Said Bobby Grich, "It was the most talented team I played on . . . . And we were a smart team, too. Everyone knew how to play the game. I couldn't wait to get to the ballpark every night. It was fun. It was exciting."

》》

Above Reggie Jackson talks with Kansas City Royals pitcher and eventual Angels pitching coach Bud Black after Jackson hit his 500th home run off of the reliever on September 17, 1985.

Right Gene Mauch was a passionate leader.

15 games and striking out 16 Mariners in one game. The highlight of the season for Witt came on the final day of the season, September 30, when he pitched the 11th perfect game in baseball history, striking out 10 and throwing just 94 pitches in a 1–0 win over the Rangers in Arlington. The victory, accomplished in just one hour and 49 minutes, leveled the Angels' season record at 81-81.

The 1984 season yielded another memorable moment when on September 17 Reggie Jackson powered his 500th career home run against future Angels pitching coach and Padres manager Bud Black of the Kansas City Royals. In typical REGGIE! fashion, there was significance and drama to the homer, occurring on the 17th anniversary of his first major league round tripper. Jackson got the ball back from his historic home run and presented it to Mauch. "I don't think you have to hit 500 home runs to get in the Hall of Fame, but it's probably a ticket in," said Reggie.

General manager Buzzie Bavasi's tenure concluded at the end of the '84 season. A colorful wheeler-dealer, Bavasi was hired by the Angels in 1977 and guided the team to its first two pennants, in '79 and '82. Buzzie, who had a long career with the Dodgers beginning in the 1930s, signed a host

Left Rod Carew, remembered most for his prowess with the bat, took great pride in his fielding at first base.

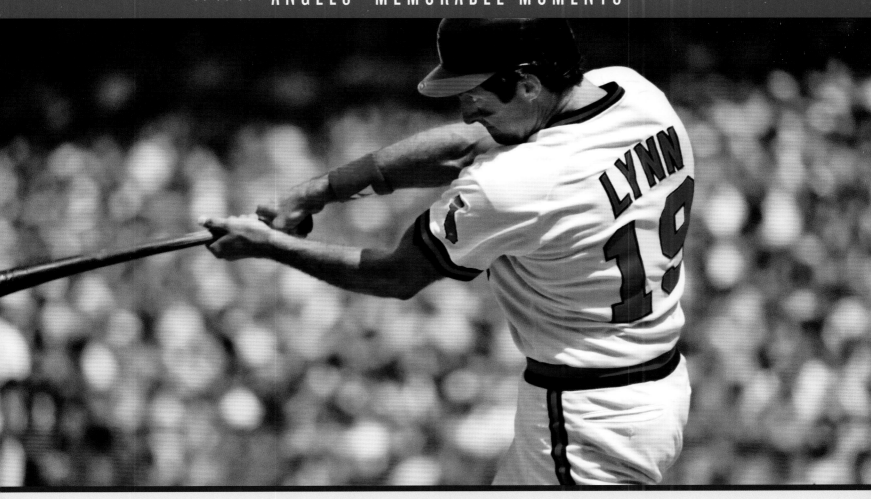

JULY 6, 1983
LYNN HITS HISTORIC GRAND SLAM IN ALL-STAR GAME

Comiskey Park, Chicago

★★

Angels center fielder Fred Lynn became the first player in the history of the All-Star Game to hit a grand slam home run when he belted one in the third inning of the annual Midsummer Classic in 1983.

San Francisco Giants ace Atlee Hammaker, a lefty who was leading the National League with a 1.70 ERA, was ordered by manager Whitey Herzog to intentionally walk Milwaukee's Robin Yount to get to the left-handed-hitting Lynn. But the Angels star lined a 2-2 sinker into the bleachers to score Yount, Rod Carew, and Manny Trillo and give the American League a 7–1 lead. The AL went on to win, 13–3, the

first win over the National League since 1971.

For Lynn, who was named the Most Valuable Player of the game, it was his ninth (and last) All-Star appearance.

The first (and only) grand slam in the history of the game wasn't the only highlight of significance. It was the 50th anniversary of the first All-Star Game and the final All-Star appearances of mainstays Carl Yastrzemski of the Red Sox and Johnny Bench of the Reds. And the first for Cal Ripken Jr. of the Orioles.

Q&A with ROD CAREW

ON THE 1982 ANGELS . . .

There was so much fun in that locker room because we knew that we could play. We knew that we could play, and we pushed each other every night that we went out there to play. No one complained about anything. We just went out and we played the game the way we knew how to play the game, and we had fun playing the game.

ON HIS UNORTHODOX SWING . . .

My swing came from a Nolan Ryan fastball. Early in my career, I used to stand with my hands higher, and when Nolan Ryan threw me a high fastball, I couldn't catch up to it. So I started experimenting with getting down a little bit lower in the crouch and trying to force him to bring the ball down. Once I started doing that, I noticed that guys who threw hard, if I allowed them to bring the ball down, the ball didn't have as much jump on it. I started getting a couple hits here and there, and I started doing better against Nolan Ryan.

ON A HITTER'S WORK ETHIC . . .

I used to take extra batting practice five, six days of the week. Why? Because I did not want to be a .220 hitter. I wanted to be way above everybody else. So I came out and worked at different things because, during the course of a ballgame, if a pitcher was getting me out one way, I wanted to be able to switch my approach. I did not want to give away at bats.

ON GENE MAUCH . . .

The first time I met Gene Mauch, I said, "Just let me play the game, and I'll run through a brick wall for you." He said, "Okay" and that was it. We developed a relationship beyond just player and manager. Gene showed up for a seven o'clock night game at eight o'clock in the morning. He had 10 or 15 different lineups going, trying to figure out strategy of which lineup he would use that night. He loved the game.

ON MIKE WITT . . .

I expected Mike Witt to throw a perfect game every time he went out to pitch because that is the kind of stuff he had. I mean, he had lights-out stuff. This guy had a great fastball, good breaking ball. He knew how to pitch. Whenever Mike pitched, I always knew the other team was in for a rough night.

Q&A with DOUG DECINCES

ON THE 1982 SEASON . . .

We had four MVPs on that team. The fans were awesome because they recognized that this team was something special. As our season started rolling, the stadium would be filled with 63,000 people. It was a pretty impressive display.

ON BOB BOONE . . .

I loved how Bob mentally controlled the game for his pitchers. Bob knew what everyone in the infield was trying to do, and we always had great communication. We always forced the double play—I mean always. And Bob was always trying to work pitches and counts to get a ground ball that we could use to turn a double play.

ON FRED LYNN . . .

I think Fred Lynn was the most natural, most gifted baseball player I played with. He didn't have the speed of Devon White or Gary Pettis, but Freddy was always there. He never made a mistake throwing to a base. He was extremely accurate mentally.

I was playing on September 21, 1982, when he and Brian Downing went flying into the outfield and Freddy went over the top of Brian to catch that ball off the wall. It was a very intense moment because our season was coming down to the line. It was a phenomenal play.

ON GENE MAUCH . . .

Gene Mauch wanted to win the game 1–0 on a squeeze bunt with two outs in the ninth inning. That was his game. He had an incredible level of intensity. If we had a game where the score was close, he had his hands on his knees right there in the front of the dugout. He played every single pitch.

ON WALLY JOYNER . . .

He was a slick-fielding first baseman and a wonderful kid. It was fun to get caught up in the "Wally World" phenomenon, and it was fun to joke with him about it. It was great to see the fans fall in love with Wally Joyner.

of big-name players like Carew and Jackson, who helped the team prosper on the field and at the gate. At the time of his death in 2008, commissioner Bud Selig said, "Buzzie was one of the game's greatest front-office executives during a period that spanned parts of six different decades. He loved the game, and he loved talking about it."

Mauch was back in the saddle again in '85, leading the Angels to 90 wins, falling just a game shy of the division title, won by Kansas City.

Carew became the 16th player in major league history and the first born out of the United States (he was born in Panama) to collect 3,000 hits when he singled off Frank Viola of the Twins on August 4, 1985. Carew, who had won seven batting titles with Minnesota, played seven seasons in Anaheim, made six All-Star teams, and batted .314.

A third Hall of Fame milestone was realized in June of '86 when 41-year-old Don Sutton would win his 300th game, pitching a three-hit complete game against Texas. Mauch had moved Sutton up in the rotation so he would have a shot at No. 300 at home.

The Angels were changing by the late '80s. Carew retired after the '85 season, Grich after the '86 season. Reggie left after '86, and Sutton after '87.

Wally World became part of Anaheim lore in '86 as rookie Wally Joyner flew into the spotlight. An All-American at BYU, Joyner was a baby-faced first baseman with a velvet swing who had worked his way through the Angels farm system after being drafted in the third round in '83.

Joyner had the unenviable task of replacing Rod Carew, but his infectious smile and clutch hitting made him a hit in the clubhouse and in the stands. By May 16, he had 15 home runs and was the talk of the baseball world. The 23-year-old Joyner and the 39-year-old Jackson made an interesting pair, as Steve Bisheff wrote in the *Orange County Register*: "They are two stars from separate galaxies, one about to fade from view after years of dazzling notoriety, the other just now twinkling into prominence."

In July, Joyner became the first rookie to be voted to a starting berth in the All-Star Game, where he tied the Mets' Darryl Strawberry in the annual home run–hitting derby.

Above Don Sutton won his 300th career game during his time with the Angels.

A third Hall of Fame milestone was realized in June of '86 when 41-year-old Don Sutton won his 300th game, pitching a three-hit complete game against Texas. Mauch had moved Sutton up in the rotation so he would have a shot at No. 300 at home.

Left Rod Carew recorded his 3,000th hit in an Angels uniform while playing against his former team, the Minnesota Twins.

Right Sutton, the 41-year-old pitcher, waves in gratitude to the fans after win number 300.

A month later, the team would stage the biggest rally in club history. Trailing the Tigers by seven runs, 12–5, in the bottom of the ninth, the Angels rewarded the fans who had stayed by scoring eight runs and winning, 13–12. Jack Howell, George Hendrick, and Bobby Grich dove in runs to cut the lead to three. Light-hitting shortstop Dick Schofield then hit a grand slam home run to win it in dramatic fashion.

Joyner and center fielder Gary Pettis represented a new generation of Angels in '86, but it would be the veterans Jackson (age 40), Sutton (41), Grich (37), Bob Boone (38), DeCinces (35), and Downing (35) who led them to another division title. Joyner, who was runner-up for Rookie of the Year, contributed 100 RBI, and Pettis added 50 steals to help push the team through a long pennant race against the Texas Rangers.

The Angels prevailed by five games and headed for the postseason against the Red Sox.

The series opened in Fenway, where Witt pitched a five-hit complete game to beat Roger Clemens as Downing drove in four runs and Joyner

> **Joyner and center fielder Gary Pettis represented a new generation of Angels in '86, but it would be the veterans Jackson (age 40), Sutton (41), Grich (37), Bob Boone (38), DeCinces (35), and Downing (35) who led them to another division title.**

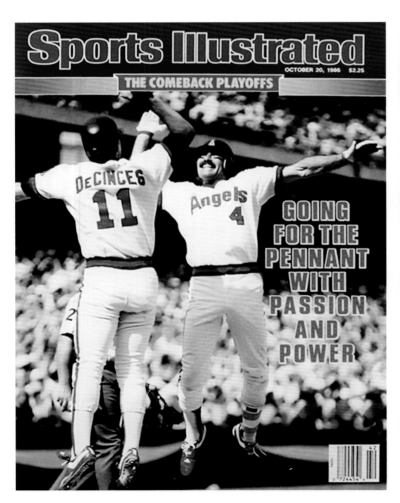

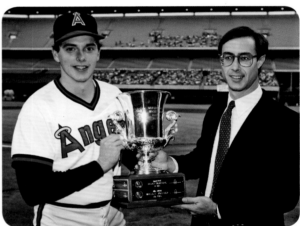

Above Doug DeCinces and Bobby Grich had a lot to celebrate in 1986.

Top Wally Joyner played in a world of his own during his rookie year and was rewarded with a starting spot in the 1986 All-Star Game.

Above Bryan Harvey, who would emerge as a dominant closer, made his big league debut in 1987.

1986 WALLY WORLD

The "Big A"

Wally Joyner, a 23-year-old cherub-faced first baseman from Utah, exploded onto the baseball scene with a fantasyland rookie season, hitting home runs and winning fans at such a rapid rate that his exploits were dubbed Wally World.

On April 9, Joyner hit his first home run off Seattle's Mark Langston in just his second game as a major leaguer. Angels fans immediately embraced the young star. Chants of WAL-LY! WAL-LY! WAL-LY! broke out during each of his at bats.

For six weeks, Joyner ruled the American League, slugging 16 home runs by May 26. He also had a knack for timely hitting to complement his surprising power. He played spectacular defense and had a wholesome, infectious smile.

Joyner became a national sensation, reaching 20 home runs by the All-Star break. He became the

first rookie ever voted as a starter in the All-Star Game. He batted third in the American League lineup and tied the Mets' Darryl Strawberry for the most home runs in the All-Star Home Run Derby.

Joyner finished 1986 with a .290 average, 22 home runs, and 100 RBI. A staph infection, suffered in early August, sapped his strength for the rest of the season. The illness required Joyner's hospitalization after Game 3 of the American League Championship Series, and he missed the rest of the series. In one of the more controversial Rookie of the Year votes, Joyner finished second to Jose Canseco of Oakland.

In 1987, Joyner hit 34 home runs and drove in 117, becoming only the ninth player in major league history to have back-to-back 100 RBI seasons at the start of his career.

Wally Joyner, the Angels' fresh-faced star, won fans with his remarkable hitting.

Q&A with WALLY JOYNER

ON HIS ROOKIE SEASON . . .

I was like a kid in a candy store, just surrounded by veterans. Our ball club had Doug DeCinces, Bobby Grich, Brian Downing, Reggie Jackson, Don Sutton, Bob Boone—just veteran after veteran. Going into Spring Training, we had six first basemen, and luckily I played well enough to make the club and get the starting spot. I also had a start that year that I never dreamed of, 17 home runs in the first 40 games.

ON ROD CAREW . . .

Rod was a professional and a perfectionist. Some people who watched Rod lay down a bunt to third base would say, "He was just lucky." But those people did not see the hours that he put in practicing and perfecting that play.

ON MEETING REGGIE JACKSON IN THE CLUBHOUSE . . .

Reggie looked at me and said, "You're a pitcher, right?" He said that because I was skinny and had no muscle tone.

I told him, "No. I'm a first baseman." Reggie started to rag on me, asking me how many home runs and RBI I had. He told me it sounded like I had a good year in AAA, and he welcomed me to the big leagues. Then he said, "Oh, by the way, my name is Reggie."

I said, "Who?" He did not know what to say, and I let him sit there for a minute. Then I said, "Mr. Jackson, you are a hero of mine. I know who you are. You were giving me a hard time, so I thought I needed to give you one back."

Reggie and I have been great friends ever since. From that point on, he really wrapped his arms around me. He would give me the scouting report on pitchers, tell me to watch out for this and look out for that. I think he was one of the best.

ON MIKE WITT . . .

Mike Witt was a joy to play behind. He was a guy that took the ball, and he was a winner. He had a desire to be in control of the game. When he took the ball, I always could feel that he was doing it for all of us, his teammates.

ON THE ANGELS ORGANIZATION . . .

The Angels will always be my favorite team. They will always be an incredible, big part of my life, and they will always be in my heart. They gave me my first chance, and I will never forget that.

Q&A with DON SUTTON

ON REGGIE JACKSON . . .

Reggie was fun to be around. He was entertaining. With Reggie, there was never any boredom. It was so easy to talk to him. If there was ever a lull in the conversation, you could bring up any number of subjects and ask Reggie, and he would give you a dissertation on it. I found him to be a good teammate. I enjoyed my time with him because he was a competitor and a tough guy to get out.

ON GARY PETTIS . . .

He played with grace, and he glided. He did not run; he wasn't elbows and everything running. He glided, and then he was there waiting for the ball to drop into his glove. Gary played like a ballet dancer with grace and elegance, and that was fun to watch.

I'll always have a special attachment to him, too, because when I came to the Angels, he came over to me and said, "I know you've always worn No. 20, so you can have it." He was an established guy, and he did not have to do that. I will always appreciate that gesture.

ON ROD CAREW . . .

I felt like every time he walked to the plate, he knew what pitch was coming. Hitters are not supposed to get inside the pitcher's head. But I would look at Rod Carew with the bat laid back on his shoulder and I say to myself, "This guy knows what's coming." He was such an artist with the bat that he made life difficult for every pitcher he faced.

ON HIS APPROACH TO THE GAME . . .

I was always looking for a way to be better and a way to stay in shape. The best baseball advice I ever got in my life came from a man who never played a day in his life, and that man was my dad. The night I left for my first Spring Training, he said, "Most of the people there are going to be better than you. But don't let anybody outwork you." I like to think that I followed that advice.

DET. 302 030 310   12 14 2
CAL. 100 002 208   13 17 1

REMEMBER TO
"BUCKLE-UP" & DRIVE SAFELY
ON YOUR WAY HOME

10:47

AUGUST 29, 1986
THE GREAT COMEBACK

The "Big A"

★★★

Trailing the Detroit Tigers by seven runs, 12–5, entering the ninth inning, the Angels staged the biggest comeback in club history, scoring eight times in the final inning for a most improbable 13–12 win.

And the unlikely offensive hero was light-hitting shortstop Dick Schofield.

Jack Howell's bases-loaded double started the rally and made it 12–7. Tiger manager Sparky Anderson called on relief ace Willie Hernandez, the AL Cy Young Award winner two years earlier. But the Angels continued the assault. George Hendrick and Bobby Grich registered RBI singles, and suddenly it was a three-run game, 12–9.

The Angels loaded the bases again, but with two out, little optimism remained in the crowd of 32,992 with Schofield, a .249 hitter, coming to bat.

But Schofield lofted a fly ball to left that fell into the bleachers for a walk-off grand slam home run and a memorable conclusion.

lined a pair of doubles in an 8–1 Angels rout. Despite a home run by Joyner in Game 2, Boston evened the series with a 9–2 win.

In Anaheim, the fans were treated to some wildly entertaining and nail-biting baseball. Pettis and Schofield homered in the bottom of the seventh in Game 3 as 64,206 roared their approval in a stunning 5–3 comeback win to put the Angels up, two games to one.

It was even more electrifying the next night when, down 3–0 to Clemens in the 8th inning, the Angels staged another pulsating rally. DeCinces homered to lead off the 9th, and after singles by Schofield and Boone, Clemens was gone. Pettis doubled in one run, and when Downing was hit by a pitch to force in a run, the game was tied. In the bottom of the 11th, Bobby Grich, playing his final season, singled to left to drive in the winning run, and the Angels were one game away from the World Series, leading the Red Sox, three games to one.

Now that elusive pennant and ticket to the World Series were within their grasp. The Angels had Witt on the mound and were home for Game 5. They built a 5–2 lead and held it until the ninth inning. It was an inning that would live in infamy for Angels fans. When Witt retired the first hitter, the count was down to two outs. The stadium held its collective breath.

But Don Baylor, the former Angels star who had left as a free agent after the '82 season, ripped a two-run home run off Witt to make it 5-4, and the anxiety level rose several notches. Witt got the second out of the inning, and Mauch, playing the percentages, brought in lefty Gary Lucas to pitch to left-handed-hitting Rich Gedman. But Lucas hit Gedman and Mauch pulled the left-hander for his bullpen ace, Donnie Moore.

Above Donnie Moore and the '86 Angels were one strike away from the World Series.

Left Donnie Moore is consoled by pitching coach Marcel Lachemann.

"The pitch...to left field and deep, and Downing goes back...and it's gone! Unbelievable! You're looking at one for the ages here. Astonishing! Anaheim Stadium was one strike away from turning into Fantasyland! And now the Red Sox lead 6–5!"

Q&A with BOB BOONE

ON THROWING OUT RUNNERS . . .

The one year I threw out a lot of runners, I had great pitchers who got the ball to the plate quickly. Geoff Zahn got it there in 1.1 seconds, and Mike Witt got it there in 1 flat. When I had that extra time, all of a sudden my mechanics got real good and the throw seemed easier.

ON HIS PITCHING STAFF . . .

I loved catching Geoff Zahn. He did not throw very hard, but he had tremendous command and a tremendous changeup. I loved catching Mike Witt, Don Sutton (I caught his 300th win), Ken Forsch, and Bruce Kison. If a pitcher was on that night, I loved catching him.

ON HIS DURABILITY AS A CATCHER . . .

To be a catcher, you have to be incredibly tough. I had to learn to play with injuries and, in some cases, serious injuries. I trained every day for 15 years. In my mind, those workouts gave me the longevity I had and the ability to set records behind the plate. To be a catcher, you really have to have a solid mind-set. I learned how to play through injuries, and that really is a skill you can learn.

ON CATCHING MIKE WITT'S PERFECT GAME . . .

We did not have much of a cushion in that game, so there was nothing said in the dugout between innings. Everybody really bit into the legend of not saying anything to the pitcher. Witt was so on, he was incredible. He had a great, unhittable curveball. He threw every pitch into my glove; I did not have to move it at all.

ON GENE MAUCH . . .

Gene Mauch without a doubt had the best baseball mind of any man I have ever been around. All his teams overachieved, and he was magnificent at getting the most out of his players. Getting to play for him, I got to learn so much about the game. He could remember everything down to counts in a game that happened years ago. He would say, "Do you remember that game we were playing when you came to bat that third time and there were two strikes on you and . . ." I mean, he remembered everything. He was remarkable.

ON BRIAN DOWNING . . .

He had a little more talent than people give him credit for. He was a real natural hitter. He became incredibly strong by lifting weights that NFL linemen were lifting. With that strength added to his swing, he started hitting the ball over the wall and did a tremendous job in the leadoff spot.

Q&A with GARY PETTIS

ON HIS SPEED . . .

I knew I had a special talent, which was my ability to run. Some guys are blessed with throwing arms, some guys are blessed with the power to hit the ball out of the park. I was blessed with speed, and if I did not use it, then it would make me just an ordinary player.

ON JIMMIE REESE . . .

Jimmie and I would always play a little game. He would try to hit balls over the outfield wall, just far enough out of my reach so that I had to really jump to even have a shot at catching them. If I caught enough, then he would buy me ice cream. If I missed enough, then I would have to buy him ice cream. We would always play that little game, and that is one of the reasons why I was very familiar with playing a ball near the wall.

ON HIS NICKNAME . . .

Jimmie Reese helped me a lot with my outfield work, and I will never forget that. He used to call me "Leather" because of the material of a baseball glove. With his help I made a lot of catches in the outfield, so he just called me "Leather."

ON BEING A SUCCESSFUL BASE STEALER . . .

I knew I had to be more than just fast. I had to be quick, sure, but I also had to be able to read a pitcher. Being able to read a pitcher is probably the most important thing to being a successful base stealer.

ON HIS TEAMMATES . . .

I looked up to everyone on our team. To be able to play Major League Baseball is something special, and it's a fraternity. I really enjoyed my time. Especially when I think about our team: We had Rod Carew, Reggie Jackson, Brian Downing, Fred Lynn, Don Baylor—the list goes on and on. It was easy for me to learn how to play the game because of the way those guys went about their business.

ON ROD CAREW . . .

He was very meticulous about what he did. He prepared extremely hard, and he was a fighter, a gamer. He did not want the opposing pitcher to beat him. That attitude rubbed off on the players around him.

Dave Henderson, who had hit just one home run for the Red Sox during the season after being acquired from Seattle, was the batter. To the shock of more than 64,000 fans, Henderson hit a fly ball into the left field bullpen, and the Red Sox had the lead, 6–5. On ABC, announcer Al Michaels said, "The pitch . . . to left field and deep, and Downing goes back . . . and it's gone! Unbelievable! You're looking at one for the ages here. Astonishing! Anaheim Stadium was one strike away from turning into Fantasyland! And now the Red Sox lead 6–5!"

That the Angels rallied in the bottom of the inning, tying the game on Rob Wilfong's single, was a credit to their resiliency. But with the bases loaded, DeCinces and Grich couldn't manage to get the winning run in, and Boston won it in the 11th on a sacrifice fly by Henderson to score Baylor.

Crushed by the loss and flat as pancakes, the Angels lost two straight in Boston, and the season was over. They would not return to the postseason for 16 years.

It was not only a decade of near misses but also one of hope and determination, personified by a remarkable young man who dazzled the entire sports world and became a symbol for undaunted courage.

He was likely the most inspirational story in Angels history—James Abbott of Flint, Michigan. Born without a right hand, Abbott nevertheless became a standout pitcher at the University of Michigan and won the 1988 Sullivan Award, emblematic of the top amateur athlete in the nation. The Angels drafted him in the first round, and he made his debut a year later, remarkably winning a dozen games.

Top Bob Boone was a stalwart catcher for the Angels.

Above Glimpse of the Future: Jim Abbott.

Left The Veteran and the Kid: Bert Blyleven clowns around with Wally Joyner.

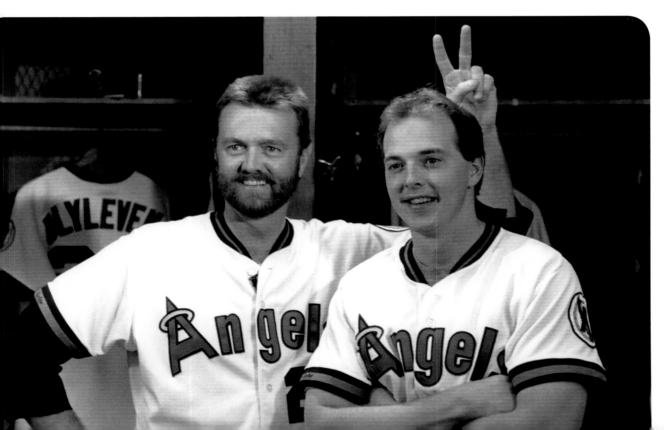

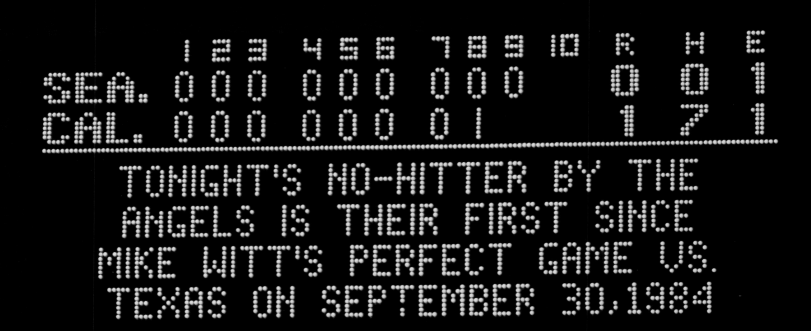

TONIGHT'S NO-HITTER BY THE ANGELS IS THEIR FIRST SINCE MIKE WITT'S PERFECT GAME VS. TEXAS ON SEPTEMBER 30,1984

APRIL 11, 1990
LANGSTON, WITT COMBINE FOR NO-HITTER

The "Big A"

★★★

Mark Langston, in his Angels debut, and veteran Mike Witt combined for a no-hitter in the third game of the 1990 season in a 1–0 win over the Seattle Mariners before a crowd of 25,632 fans.

It was only the fifth time in major league history that pitchers had combined for a no-hitter.

Langston, who had signed as a free agent during the off-season, worked the first seven innings, walking four, striking out three, and throwing 99 pitches. Due to a work stoppage there had been an abbreviated Spring Training, so the pitch count for the newest Angel was of concern, and manager Doug Rader removed him.

The Angels scored their only run of the game on a bases-loaded walk to Dante Bichette in the seventh.

Witt, who had been a mainstay in the starting rotation for nine years but was now operating out of the bullpen, picked up for Langston in the eighth inning. The big righty, who would be traded to the Yankees for outfielder Dave Winfield the following month, was on his game, retiring Edgar Martinez and Greg Briley on groundouts and striking out Dave Valle.

In the ninth, pinch hitter Scott Bradley and Harold Reynolds each grounded out to second, bringing Ken Griffey Jr. to the plate as Seattle's last chance. On a 2-2 pitch, Griffey swung and missed, completing the Angels' eighth no-hitter and their first involving more than one pitcher.

Mike Witt, the Angels ace of the '80s, begins the '90s by combining for a no-hitter with Mark Langston, the pitcher of the next decade.

Q&A with MIKE WITT

ON GROWING UP AN ANGELS FAN . . .

I would go to games and sit in the upper deck for a few bucks or whatever it was back in the mid-'60s. In the '70s, when I was 10 or 11 years old, I started really getting into the games. I would watch Ryan and Tanana pitch back to back, and that is what got my juices going as far as me wanting to become a baseball player.

ON HIS SUPERSTITIONS . . .

I always went to warm up before the game with one stick of Carefree bubble gum. Why not Bazooka? I don't know. I also drank half a cup of coffee before every game. Only half a cup. I never stepped on the white line when walking on or walking off the field. I had those three things going before every game I pitched.

ON DON BAYLOR . . .

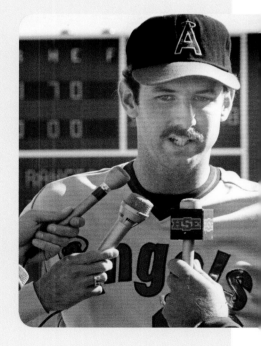

Don was the best teammate I ever had. He took me under his wing when I was a rookie, and I really appreciated it at the time and throughout the rest of my career, too. Everybody looked up to Don Baylor. Whatever he said came from his heart, and you knew you should take it to heart, too, because he was not just going to say something to you for the sake of saying it. He meant everything he said.

ON BOB BOONE . . .

Bob Boone really helped me when I was a young pitcher. Getting to throw to him in my second year, he steered my career in the right direction all the way through. I started throwing to him when I was 22, and I threw to him until I was 28. For that period of my playing time, I could not have thrown to a better catcher.

ON GARY PETTIS . . .

Gary Pettis was a human highlight film. He could get his body over the fence and bring it back. He probably brought back five or six of my pitches that should have been home runs. He was a gamer. He came to play every day, and if the ball was in the air, he had a chance of catching it.

ON HIS PERFECT GAME . . .

It was the last day of season. That is the first thing I remember about it. The other thing that comes to my mind is that my wife happened to be there. She was the only wife on the road trip that day. That game was a culmination of my first really good year in the big leagues. That win gave me 15 wins for the season, and it propelled me into four more really good years. It gave me a lot of confidence and made me realize that I belonged.

Downing, who switched from catcher to outfielder and eventually designated hitter, was productive throughout the decade, hitting 20 or more home runs six of seven years. Boone, who took over behind the plate, won four Gold Gloves.

Things were hardly dull around Anaheim in 1989 with the addition of Bert Blyleven to the rotation. A fun-loving veteran who grew up in Orange County just minutes from the stadium, he was 38 years old and thought to be finished. But he carved out what might have been the best season of his illustrious career, going 17-5 with a 2.73 ERA and a league-leading five shutouts to earn American League Comeback Player of the Year honors.

The decade closed in 1989 with a terrific All-Star Game, the second one hosted by the Angels. The dynamic multisport star Bo Jackson of the Royals, who would later play for the Angels, led off the bottom of the first inning with a monstrous 448-foot home run to center field that landed halfway up the tarps, and Wade Boggs of the Red Sox would follow with another one. Bo added a run-scoring single, a stolen base, and a magnificent catch in the outfield as the AL scored a 5–3 victory before a huge crowd of 64,036. Jackson was the MVP. The fans were further delighted that one of their favorites, Nolan Ryan (then pitching for the Texas Rangers), was the winning pitcher.

Above Brian Downing's workout regimen kept him healthy and fit to play three different positions with the Angels.

Below Bert Blyleven was known for his abilities on the mound and his antics off the field.

Above Blyleven threw five shutouts in 1989, leading the league.

CHAPTER 4: 1990s

CHANGING TIMES

The winds of change came sweeping through Anaheim in the 1990s. In 1996, the Walt Disney Company purchased a part interest (25 percent) in the team with the agreement they would become sole owners upon the passing of Gene Autry. Jackie Autry, Gene's wife, had been in charge of the day-to-day operations of the team for some time. With Disney on the scene, she relinquished those responsibilities to the company. The Disney purchase was hailed as beneficial for the franchise, the city of Anaheim, and Orange County. Any concerns about the Angels' future stability were laid to rest.

"Disney had a longtime history here, of course," said Tom Daly, the mayor of Anaheim at the time. "They were an experienced, sophisticated, and competitive organization. They also brought a sense of that celebrity tone to the purchase that the Angels had with Mr. Autry. The ultimate result of Disney's purchase was the rebuilding of the stadium and the world championship in 2002."

Added Jim Ruth, the Anaheim city manager, "There was talk of the team being moved to South Orange County if it was sold to another group, so we were delighted that Disney stepped in. Jackie Autry felt strongly about keeping the team here. Of course, the team has a tremendous economic and social benefit to our community. They have always been huge influences in all they do for charity."

Disney changed the name of the team to the Anaheim Angels, introduced a new team logo—a periwinkle plate and crossed bats—and sold the stadium naming rights to Southern California Edison (thus Edison International Field).

Earlier in the decade, the Los Angeles Rams, who had been cotenants since 1980, moved from Anaheim in 1994, and the stadium was reconfigured, at a cost of $118 million ($20 million from the city of Anaheim; the remainder was paid by Disney), to baseball size once again (going from a capacity of 65,150 to 45,050).

Disney's purchase of the team ensured that the Angels would remain in Orange County and Anaheim would continue to be the sports capital of the region.

They also brought a sense of that celebrity tone to the purchase that the Angels had with Mr. Autry. The ultimate result of Disney's purchase was the rebuilding of the stadium and the World Championship in 2002.

Left Hitting coach Rod Carew is recognized by his pupils.

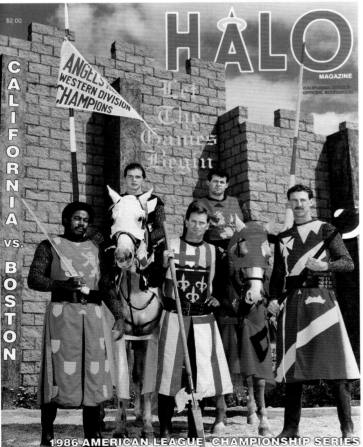

Top Carew (bottom right) and his offense enjoyed some record-setting performances in 1995.

Above Jim Abbott and Jimmie Reese.

Right Abbott was a fan favorite from Day One.

ON JIMMIE REESE . . .

Jimmie Reese was the kindest man I ever met. He just lit up whatever room, or dugout, or outfield he was in. Just his smile—it was infectious. It didn't matter who he was with or where he was at, he could charm anybody. He really took me under his wing, and I would sit and spend time with him, and he'd tell me stories of his playing days. I spent a lot of time in the outfield with Jimmie and that sawed-off fungo bat of his. He would hit balls at me, and I really think that helped me become a much better fielder at the major league level. I had to go through my motion with the glove and follow through, and he had perfect timing, like the timing on the field, which is very hard to replicate. We did that every day, and it really helped me.

ON CHUCK FINLEY . . .

I cannot think of any other teammate that I would rather have in my corner than Chuck Finley. I mean that in any situation, personally or athletically. He is just a wonderfully strong and loyal person. He was always a fun-loving guy, but his approach on the field was incredible. There was a seriousness to the way Chuck approached the game.

ON TIM SALMON, JIM EDMONDS, AND GARRET ANDERSON . . .

They just had a lot of confidence. Tim Salmon was a hard-working guy just loaded with talent. Jimmy Edmonds just gave out this aura of confidence: He was going to make the catch, he was going to get the hit. Garret was the same in a sort of quiet way. He had that same "I know I can do this" kind of feeling.

ON THE ANGELS FANS . . .

The Angels fans treated me magnificently. I can never fully express my appreciation for how I was received there. Everywhere I went in the organization, everyone was so supportive and so great. I loved being a part of this team. I really looked at the Angels as my baseball family. To this day I consider them the team that I root for, the team that I follow, the team that I'm close with.

ON THE 1991 TEAM . . .

We had a great, healthy competition between everyone on the pitching staff. Having Chuck and Mark and Kirk McCaskill and Marcel Lachemann as our pitching coach—one of my favorite people in the world—we had a lot of pride in our staff. We worked hard. Every one of those guys, to a man, were the hardest-working pitchers I ever played with.

ON MIKE WITT . . .

Mike Witt was one of the hardest-working guys I've ever seen in my life. I knew it was just a different ballgame when I saw him pitch. I just said, "Wow." I never thought about lifting this kind of weight or running those stairs to get better until I played with Mike.

Right Autry enjoyed the accomplishments of his players, such as Reggie Jackson's 500th career home run.

Bottom Right Don Baylor, the first Angels MVP, and Autry, during Angels Hall of Fame induction ceremonies.

Above Gene Autry celebrates at the ballpark with general manager Fred Haney.

"He loved the game and was always around the clubhouse, especially in those early days," said Jim Fregosi. "When I managed Philadelphia in the World Series in 1993, Gene called me before every game to wish me well."

On October 2, 1998, Gene Autry, the beloved owner of the team, died. The death of Autry, one of the most popular figures in the history of the game, hit everyone hard.

JIM FREGOSI: "He was special, no doubt about it. A great guy and a great friend. He loved the game and was always around the clubhouse, especially in those early days. When I managed Philadelphia in the World Series in 1993, Gene called me before every game to wish me well."

BOBBY GRICH: "He loved his players as if we were his sons."

BOBBY WINKLES: "You couldn't work for a nicer man. He wrote me a handwritten note when I was fired and told me he was sorry it didn't work out."

DEAN CHANCE: "Nobody ever said a bad word about Mr. Autry. He was a wonderful and nice person."

ROD CAREW: "He was the kind of man you could just sit down and talk to. And he did it with all the players, rookies and veterans, stars and subs. He was a very impressive man."

CLYDE WRIGHT: "He was a person that everyone had respect for. And he always came to the locker room and talked to all the guys. He knew our wives' names and our kids' names. He was quite a man."

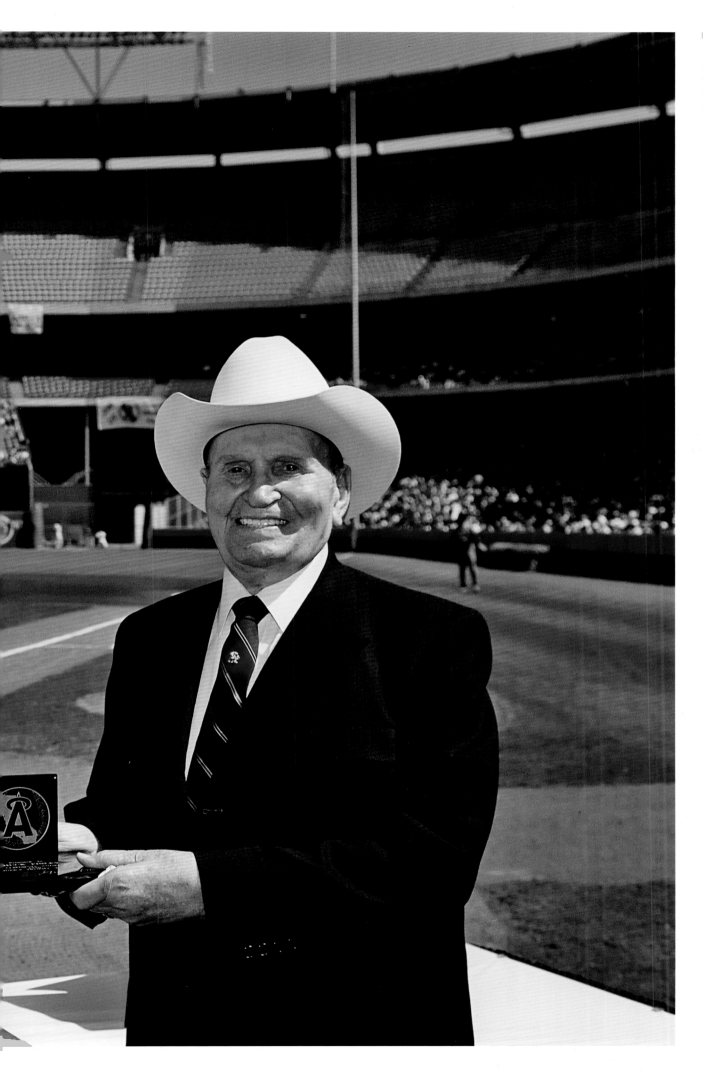

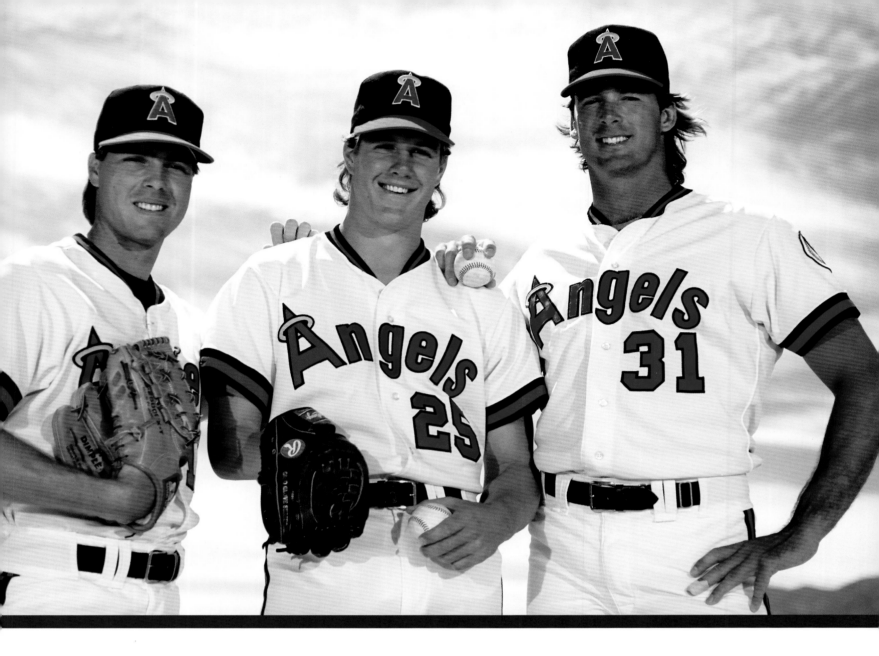

On the field, the Angels, for the first time since the '60s, failed to reach the postseason at least once in the decade, although they came tantalizing close.

Once again, there was no shortage of star power.

The Angels sported a trio of talented left-handed pitchers who, in 1991, combined for 55 wins (against only 28 losses). Mark Langston won 19, Chuck Finley 18, and Jim Abbott 18. One of the strongest pitching staffs the Angels had ever produced also featured closer Bryan Harvey, who saved 46 games and posted an ERA of 1.60.

Far Left Mark Langston, in his Angel debut, combined with Mike Witt for a no-hitter, the eighth in club history.

Left Langston and first baseman J. T. Snow are recognized with Gold Gloves trophies, two of six they totaled between them with the Angels.

Left Teammates on the field and best of friends off, left-handers Langston, Jim Abbott, and Chuck Finley.

Below Bryan Harvey recorded a dominant 1991 season with an American League–leading 46 saves, in addition to a 1.60 ERA.

Finley, a tall (six foot six) and graceful lefty from Louisiana, was evolving into the ace of the staff. Combining a devastating split-finger fastball with a forkball, he went 52-27 from '89 to '91 and finished his career in Anaheim with the most wins in team history, 165. Langston was also one of the games' finest fielding pitchers, and he won five Gold Gloves during the decade. He partnered with Mike Witt to pitch a no-hitter in 1990; Langston, in his first appearance for the Angels, went the first seven innings, and Witt the final two.

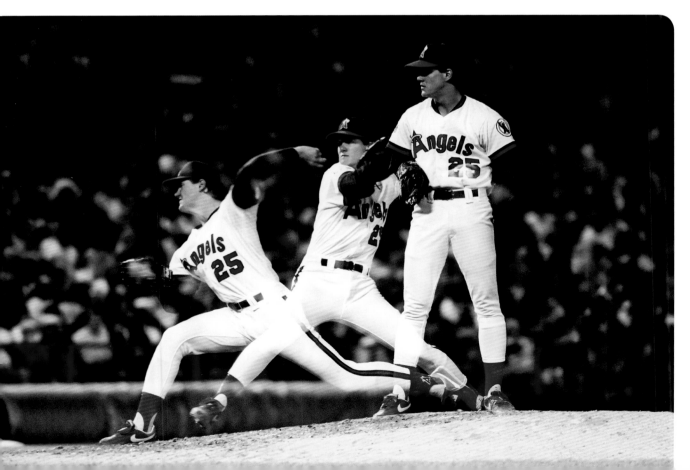

Above Louisiana native Finley was as intense on the mound as he was easygoing off it.

Left Abbott bypassed the minor leagues, making the big league club straight out of his first Spring Training.

ON JOINING THE ANGELS . . .

The Angels were a team I really wanted to be a part of. I always loved coming to Angel Stadium to pitch. It was always one of my favorite ballparks because the fans were great, the atmosphere was great. They were a team that I knew would give me an opportunity to contend. That's all I really asked for as a player, so it was a perfect fit for me.

ON HIS FIRST START FOR THE ANGELS IN 1990 . . .

That year we only had three weeks of Spring Training. I pitched about four innings a game, and so I had not really been stretched out properly. It was a bizarre game because of that. I walked a ton of guys and threw a bunch of pitches. I was only supposed to throw five innings, but I ended up going to the seventh. At that point, I was done. I was out of gas. So Mike Witt came in, and we ended up combining on a no-hitter.

ON DARIN ERSTAD . . .

Darin was an absolute throwback to the way the game is supposed to be played. I love guys who show up every day and who work very hard in the off-season, who train real hard and take this game so seriously, guys who are willing to do whatever it takes to win, and Darin would do whatever it took to win a baseball game.

ON JIMMIE REESE . . .

When Jimmie sat in our dugout, the history of the game was sitting with us. To this day, being able to sit with that guy night after night is the best thing that happened to me playing the game of baseball. Here he was, 92 years old, hitting us fungos. He could put some little topspin on his fungos that made them hard to field. Whenever I made an error on one of those, I looked up and Jimmie would be laughing at me, having a great time.

ON HIS TEAMMATES . . .

We had a lot of veteran guys, and every night 8 or 10 of us would sit around and talk baseball after the game. I learned more sitting there listening to Chili Davis talk about his approach to hitting than I ever could have from scouting or watching film.

I remember Gary DiSarcina when he was a rookie. We invited him to listen to us talk, but we said, "Here's the deal, kid: big ears, little mouth. We don't want to hear one word from you, but you listen to these conversations." He nodded his head, "Okay, okay." It was a great learning process for everybody.

ON CHUCK FINLEY . . .

Chuck is the funniest guy I've been around in my entire life. He's always had the ability to diffuse any pressure. There's always pressure in the major leagues, and you need teammates that can diffuse it. Chuck was always perfect at that.

Above Rod Carew instructs Chili Davis on hitting, a skill he refined into an art form during his Hall of Fame career.

But the Angels got little from their offense during those years. In '92, they could only manage 88 home runs as a team. Reinforcements were on the way, though.

Garret Anderson, a smooth-swinging left-handed hitting outfielder from Kennedy High School in the San Fernando Valley, was drafted by the Angels on June 16, 1990. He would break into the Angel lineup in 1995 and remain a solid offensive contributor for the next 14 seasons, hitting better than .300 six times and driving in more than 100 runs four times. Anderson would finish his career with team records in games (2,013), runs (1,024), hits (2,368), and runs batted in (1,292). In 2003, he was both the MVP and the Home Run Derby champion of the annual MLB All-Star game, held that year at Chicago's U.S. Cellular Field.

In 1993, a Paul Bunyan in cleats burst onto the scene. An outfielder with an all-American smile and a powerful bat, Tim Salmon was drafted out of tiny Grand Canyon University in Arizona. A star from the outset, Salmon won Rookie of the Year honors in '93 (the only Angel ever to do so) by hitting 31 home runs and driving in 95.

"It was an exciting and fun time," said Salmon. "We had a lot of young guys, and the expectations weren't too high, so we just went out and played."

They had also re-signed free agent Chili Davis, who had played with the club in the late '80s. The switch-hitting Davis added 27 homers and drove in 112 in the first of four more productive seasons in Anaheim.

"It was an exciting and fun time," said Salmon. "We had a lot of young guys, and the expectations weren't too high, so we just went out and played."

Right J. T. Snow and Tim Salmon brought some spark to the early-'90s lineups.

Far Right Hailed as a top prospect, Salmon delivered the Angels' first Rookie of the Year performance in 1993.

1993
TIM SALMON:
ROOKIE OF THE YEAR

★★★

Angels outfielder Tim Salmon was a unanimous selection as the American League Rookie of the Year for 1993 after hitting 31 home runs and driving in 95 runs.

The 24-year-old Salmon hit .283 with 35 doubles and 93 runs scored. He was particularly dangerous at Anaheim Stadium, where he hit 23 home runs and batted .314.

Salmon finished his career 16 years later as the franchise leader in home runs (299), runs scored (983), walks (965), and slugging percentage (.499).

He is the only Angel to ever secure Rookie of the Year honors.

ON THE 1986 TEAM . . .

We had some characters. We had anybody from Don Sutton to John Candelaria to Reggie Jackson. They knew what they were doing. I got a lot of knowledge and experience from playing with those guys. They taught me a lot about the game, about how to play it and about how to treat it with respect.

ON GOING STRAIGHT FROM CLASS A BALL TO THE MAJOR LEAGUES . . .

I thought they had called the wrong person. When our general manager called me, I was somewhere in Iowa. He said, "We are going to need you in New York."

I said, "Do we have a AAA team in New York?"

"No, we are bringing you up to the big leagues."

"Are you sure you've got the right guy?"

"Well, I'm pretty sure we do, but if you want, we can call someone else."

I said, "No, no. I'm good with it, I'm good with it."

ON THE 1989 ALL-STAR GAME AT ANGEL STADIUM . . .

The stadium was enclosed with a bowl, so it seemed like 90,000 fans, maybe more, were there cheering us on. It was very loud, almost as loud as it was when we were in the playoffs in '86. That All-Star atmosphere was so unique, especially since it was my first time being on the team. I absorbed so much of the players and the experience because it was all so new.

ON JIM ABBOTT . . .

When Abbott came to Spring Training, there was really nothing to indicate that he was going to make the team. But he pitched his way onto the team. I mean, he outpitched everybody else that was trying for that fourth or fifth starting spot. When his first start came, it was a packed house. It was a very special moment.

ON HIS 1989 SEASON . . .

I was trying to get a third pitch together, and one of our pitching coaches taught me how to throw a split-finger fastball. It ended up being a very good pitch for me.

The coach just handed me the ball and said, "Chuck, you know you've done all the work that you need to do, and we need to put you out here for a full year and let you grow into this and see what happens."

So they threw me out there and let me go through the whole way. I started getting more comfortable with it. The next year, as soon as Spring Training kicked off, I had a sense that I belonged. Something just clicked.

Above Jim Edmonds receives one of the two Gold Gloves he would earn during his Angels career.

Below Outfielders Garret Anderson, Edmonds, and Tim Salmon.

A third young player, Jim Edmonds, joined Salmon and Anderson as regulars in the outfield in '95. Edmonds homered 33 times that year and hit 25 or more home runs each of the next three seasons while making numerous highlight-reel catches in center field.

The '95 team was the best Angels club of the decade. Behind their young outfielders Salmon and Edmonds, they built a 10½-game lead in August and were still up 6 in mid-September. But a pair of 9-game losing streaks pushed the Angels back into second before they reeled off five straight victories, two behind the pitching of Finley, to force a 1-game playoff against the Mariners. In Seattle, they ran into Randy Johnson, who throttled the Angels hitters in a 9–1 Mariner win that eliminated the Angels from the race. The loss of shortstop Gary DiSarcina, an All-Star that season, to a midseason injury proved too much for the team to overcome.

"It wasn't that we played so poorly," said Salmon. "We ran into some good teams and good pitchers. We had to face Roger Clemens twice in one home stand because of a rainout. We just got some bad matchups and then had to face the best pitcher in baseball that season in Johnson."

Salmon would finish with 34 homers and 105 RBI, while Edmonds had 33 and 107.

JULY 29, 1997

CHUCK FINLEY BECOMES ANGELS' ALL-TIME LEADER IN WINS

Jacobs Field, Cleveland

Chuck Finley won his 139th game as an Angel, surpassing Nolan Ryan's career total of 138, in a 7–2 win over the Indians.

A five-time All-Star, Finley ended his Angels' career with 165 wins—a record that still stands.

In front of 42,975 at Jacobs Field, Finley upped his record to 10-6 on the season as Jack Howell homered twice. Finley allowed just three hits in a complete game victory, striking out nine and walking two.

Finley, who won 10 or more games for the Angels 10 times in his career, finished '97 with a 13-6 record.

For the first time in American League history, one team boasted four players with 30 or more home runs: (from left) Troy Glaus, Garret Anderson, with hitting coach Mickey Hatcher (center), Mo Vaughn, and Tim Salmon.

JUNE 10, 1997
JIM EDMONDS: "THE CATCH"

Kauffman Stadium, Kansas City

★ ★

In the fifth inning of a 1–1 tie, the Royals' David Howard came to the plate with two on and two out. Howard lined a Jason Dickson fastball to straight-away center field on a line. Edmonds, who often played a shallow center, turned, put his head down, and charged back to where his instincts told him the ball might land.

As the ball sailed over his head, Edmonds threw his body in the air and blindly reached out his gloved hand as far as possible to catch the ball. He wound up on the edge of the warning track, rolling onto his back with his legs in the air, left hand reaching up to display the ball.

"That was one of the greatest plays ever," veteran umpire Dave Phillips told the *Kansas City Star*. "That made Willie Mays' play look routine."

Edmonds later doubled in the go-ahead run, and the Angels won the game, 6–2.

Edmonds won a Gold Glove that season, the first of eight he would win over a nine-year span.

That year, the Angels made Darin Erstad, a multisport star from the University of Nebraska, the No. 1 overall pick in the amateur draft. Erstad, a punter on the Cornhuskers' NCAA-championship football team as well as a baseball standout, quickly proved his value both offensively and defensively, thus forcing the Angels to employ a four-headed "monster" in the outfield. Edmonds would eventually be shipped to St. Louis in 2000 in a trade that brought Adam Kennedy to Anaheim.

In 1996 the Angels used 54 players: 25 position players and 29 pitchers. They also had three different managers—Marcel Lachemann, John McNamara, and Joe Maddon.

They climbed back into the pennant race in '97, winning 84 games to finish second in the West. Salmon had another huge year, hitting 33 homers and driving in a career-best 129 runs, while Troy Percival saved 27 games out of the bullpen.

A converted catcher, Percival was an overpowering force on the mound. He would glower down at the opponent, give a high leg kick, and deliver wicked fastballs and sliders.

Percival put up eye-popping numbers in his 10 years as the Angels closer. He saved 316 games, but even more astonishing was striking out 680 batters while allowing just 393 hits in 586 innings.

In '98, Percival saved his 42nd game of the season on September 20, a 3–1 win over Seattle, to move the club into a first-place tie with the Mariners. But Texas swept the Angels, who could manage only three runs over three games, in Anaheim, and the team finished second, three games behind the Rangers.

"It wasn't that we played so poorly," said Salmon. "We ran into some good teams and good pitchers. We had to face Roger Clemens twice in one home stand because of a rainout. We just got some bad matchups and then had to face the best pitcher in baseball that season in Johnson."

Below Converted catcher Troy Percival became the Angels' dominant closer.

Q&A with BERT BLYLEVEN

ON MARK LANGSTON . . .

When I think of Mark Langston, I think of a great competitor. He is a guy that put a lot of hard work into trying to go out there and be consistent, and he was. He had a great fastball and a great breaking ball. He went right at hitters. He was a great, great pitcher.

ON JIM ABBOTT . . .

I admire Jim Abbott for what he stands for and for what he had to go through. I admire him for the determination and the guts he had to get to the major leagues. I cannot describe how proud I am to have played with him. He is an incredible human being.

ON GROWING UP AN ANGELS FAN . . .

My friends and I used to go to the stadium and ask the ticket holders if they had any extra tickets, and that was our way of getting in without paying. I got to watch guys like Jim Fregosi and Buck Rodgers and pitchers like Clyde Wright. To watch those players compete was a great learning tool for me. That was how I spent my summers, watching the Angels play.

ON ROD CAREW . . .

I cannot name anybody in the game that had a more beautiful swing than Rod Carew. He is a very humble guy, and he's a guy that liked to have fun. But he knew as a ballplayer that his job was to hit, and that is what he did. I remember he told me once, "Certain pitchers, when they release the ball, it looks like a beach ball to me." And I thought, "No wonder he hits so well." He took a lot of pride in his defense, too. He went about his business the right way and was always a true professional.

ON BECOMING A PITCHER . . .

In Little League, I started out as a catcher. One day, our coach, Mr. Price, saw that I was throwing the ball back to the pitcher harder than he was throwing it to me. So he said, "Bert, do you want to pitch?" I said I would give it a try, and I did, and I fell in love with that baseball.

ON THE ANGELS ORGANIZATION . . .

I am very proud of what Arte Moreno is doing with the organization. I love Mike Scioscia, and I think he is a great manager. The Angels have always been a classy organization, and I was very fortunate to spend four years in an Angels uniform. I still am very proud of that.

Never bashful when it came to free-agent shopping, the Angels gave Boston Red Sox slugger Mo Vaughn the most lucrative contract in major league history (at the time) after the '98 season. Vaughn, three years removed from an MVP season and one of the game's most feared sluggers, signed a six-year, $80 million deal. While his power numbers were solid (33 homers and 108 RBI in '99 and 36 homers and 117 RBI in 2000), he did not provide the kind of thunder he had in Boston and, after missing the '01 season with an injury, was shipped to the New York Mets for pitcher Kevin Appier.

Following a subpar '99 season when the team fell from 85 wins the previous season to only 70, manager Terry Collins resigned in early September.

Baylor, Carew, Ryan, and Reese were all inducted into the Angels' Hall of Fame during the decade, joining Bobby Grich and Jim Fregosi. And in '99, the team retired Carew's No. 29.

This Page Nolan Ryan returns to Angel Stadium, the place where he established himself as one of baseball's premier pitchers. The Angels honored Ryan's accomplishments by retiring his number and inducting him into the team's Hall of Fame.

This Page Rod Carew is honored by the organization for his numerous accomplishments, including his 3,000th hit. He became the fourth member of the Angels Hall of Fame, and his number 29 is one of six retired by the club.

Garret Anderson (third from right) keeps things loose during Spring Training in Tempe, Arizona.

CHAPTER 5: 2000s

CHAMPIONS

Bill Stoneman had taken over as the Angels' ninth general manager in the fall of 1999. Stoneman was bright, friendly, and energetic. He knew what he wanted, and he set out to build teams that would regularly contend for championships.

A former major league pitcher (he had thrown two no-hitters with the Montreal Expos), Stoneman made a number of savvy acquisitions, including Chone Figgins, David Eckstein, Maicer Izturis, 2004 league MVP Vladimir Guerrero, and 2005 Cy Young Award winner Bartolo Colon.

Stoneman showed rare multiple skills in building the Angels. In players like Figgins and Izturis, he found gems in trades that appeared to be almost afterthoughts, but ones that produced valuable performers. He got players like Eckstein and Brendan Donnelly off waivers and reached into the Dominican Republic to sign Ervin Santana and Erick Aybar. At the same time, he was amazingly effective in luring big-name free agents like Colon and Guerrero to Anaheim.

But none of those had as much of a long-term effect on the franchise as Stoneman's choice as manager: Mike Scioscia.

Born in Upper Darby, Pennsylvania, a suburb south of Philadelphia, Scioscia was raised in a tough, loving atmosphere where hard work and perseverance were praised and excuses were not tolerated.

An excellent athlete, Scioscia excelled at baseball and became a first-round draft choice of the Los Angeles Dodgers in 1976. He was 18. Not surprisingly, Scioscia was a catcher. A rock-solid catcher.

He made it to the major leagues by 1980 and was basically the Dodgers' catcher for the next dozen years. Scioscia made two All-Star teams, caught a pair of no-hitters, played on two World Championship teams, and was behind the plate a team-record 1,395 times. His trademark was his uncanny ability to block home plate like a tank, discouraging runners from a collision.

But as natural as he was as a big-league catcher, his true calling came in 2000 when Angels general manager Bill Stoneman appointed him the 17th manager in club history.

A calming, steadying presence enveloped the clubhouse, and success followed. Scioscia's mantra was, "I want our team to contend, not compete. Compete is hope, but we expect to contend and expect to be a championship-caliber club."

"I sought someone I thought would have the ability to bring the club together," said Stoneman. "Someone who would have a presence with the players, with the fans, with the organization. He's a very competitive guy. He's seen the game from the players' side of it. That gives him instant credibility with the players."

In his first 10 seasons, he guided the team into the playoffs six times, more than the total number of times the franchise had reached the postseason in its first 39 years. In a six-year period from 2004 to 2009, the Angels finished first five times

Scioscia's mantra was, "I want our team to contend, not compete. Compete is hope, but we expect to contend and expect to be a championship-caliber club."

and averaged 94.5 wins per season. In 2002, the Angels, under Scioscia, climbed to the top of the baseball world by winning the World Championship, the only one in the first 50 years of club history. Twice he has been named American League Manager of the Year, although there are those who believe he deserved it on other occasions as well.

Scioscia's first team, in 2000, had plenty of firepower. Troy Glaus, the 23-year-old six-foot-five third baseman from UCLA, set a club record and led the league with 47 home runs; Mo Vaughn hit 36, Garret Anderson 35, and Tim Salmon 34. It was the first time in the history of the American League four players on the same team had hit 30 or more homers in a season. And the 236 hits that season are a club record.

It would be hard to find a more remarkable single season in Angels history than the one Darin Erstad fashioned in 2000. Erstad was all grit. He wore dirt as a badge of honor and hustled as if it was a privilege, one that he could lose if not executed at a breakneck speed at all times.

He led the American League in hits with 240 and posted career highs in almost every statistical category: runs (121), home runs (25), RBI (100 as the leadoff hitter), doubles (39), triples (6), walks (64), stolen bases (28), and batting average (.355, second in the league). He won a Gold Glove for his play in center field. It was the first of two Gold Gloves Erstad won as an outfielder, and he would go on to win a third, this time at first base, becoming the only player in history to win the fielding-excellence award at two different positions.

But despite Erstad's seminal season and the power-packed lineup, the pitching was not equal to the task, and the Angels were barely over .500 at 82-80.

Although Glaus hit 41 more home runs in '01, the club slumped to 75-87.

Above Darin Erstad, pictured here after his memorable home run in Game 6 of the 2002 World Series, defined hustle and grit and was a leader for the Angels.

Q&A with TROY GLAUS

ON MIKE SCIOSCIA . . .

He played a fun style of baseball. He took advantage of our strengths and really helped us become better players. He taught us to go beyond just going out and hitting and catching and throwing. He focused on a particular style of play: pitching, defense, aggressive base running.

ON THE 2000 TEAM . . .

I made a combination of adjustments that year and had gained a lot of experience, knowing the pitchers I was hitting against. Those factors all helped me get better as a player, but I also got better by just being in our lineup. Hitting is very contagious, and we had guys that were hitting homers and stealing bases, and it all just kind of funneled down to everyone else and helped us all have great years.

ON THE 2002 PLAYOFFS . . .

I don't think we were the most talented team in those playoffs. But we were playing the best at the time, and it was as good a run as I've seen a team have for a month. Our offense, our pitching, our defense: Everything just clicked at the right time. I knew once we were in the playoffs that anything could happen, and we were clicking on all cylinders for the whole month. It was a run I'll never forget.

ON THE WORLD SERIES VICTORY CELEBRATION . . .

It was the culmination of nine months of work. Knowing that we had just won our last game of the year and that nobody could take it away from us felt so thrilling. We were the last ones standing.

ON VLADIMIR GUERRERO . . .

He's one of the best players I've ever seen. There is no doubt about it. He does things with the bat that most people cannot do, and he has done it really well for a long time.

ON BEING A PART OF THE ANGELS . . .

The weather is as nice as it gets, and it's also a first-class organization. Starting with the front office at the top and working all the way down. They do everything to make the players as comfortable as possible. I will always remember being a part of that organization and being in that clubhouse. And I will remember it fondly.

Above Troy Glaus led the team with 30 home runs during the 2002 season.

But 2002 proved to be the most magical of seasons. The Angels fielded an incredibly balanced team. Glaus led the team in home runs (30), Anderson in RBI (123), sparkplug shortstop David Eckstein in runs (107), and second baseman Adam Kennedy in batting average (.312). Veterans contributed, with 34-year-old Kevin Appier winning 14 games, as did rookies, with 23-year-old John Lackey winning 9 and 20-year-old Francisco Rodriguez in the wings, awaiting his call to duty in the postseason.

The team won at home (54-27) and on the road (45-36). They won in the first half (51-35) and in the second half (48-28). After a slow April—in fact, the slowest in club history—6-13 and 10½ games out of first on April 23, they had a winning record in each of the next five months.

The diminutive Eckstein hit grand slam home runs on consecutive days later in April, and the unexpected power prowess ignited the team. In May, they won 14 of 16 to climb within 4 games of the lead. When Lackey won his first major league game on the last day of June in a 5-1 decision against the Dodgers, the Angels were 3½ out of first. They caught Seattle in late July with an 8–0 win over the Mariners and remained in the hunt throughout the rest of the season.

They didn't win the division, though, finishing behind the Oakland A's by 4 games with a 99-63 record. But the playoffs would prove to be all red.

It was ironic that the 2002 Angels didn't even win the division, advancing to the playoffs as the American League wild-card team.

It was a team that was better than the sum of its parts. It was a team that got major contributions from everyone on the roster. It was a team that passed around the spotlight effortlessly and frequently.

Far Left Tim Salmon celebrates the Angels' first American League Pennant.

Left and Right The Angels had many occasions to celebrate in 2002.

Far Left Adam Kennedy developed into an outstanding defensive second baseman.

Left John Lackey made a strong impression as a rookie starter in 2002.

195

ON THE 2002 SEASON . . .

We struggled in the beginning of the season. Troy Percival and Darin Erstad called a team meeting and told us, "We are better than this." The next day, we went out and won by a score of 10–1. From that point forward, we started to believe in ourselves. We knew no one else believed what we could do, so we had to go prove it to them.

ON HIS BACK-TO-BACK GRAND SLAMS, APRIL 27 AND 28, 2002 . . .

On April 28, I had gone 0-6, and the game went into extra innings. I was actually just trying to get a hit and, fortunately, the ball went out. The day before, I came up with the bases loaded, same situation. I had never done that in my career, but it was just one of those things during the season that everyone stepped up and gave us some big victories, and at that point in time, those two grand slams were my contribution.

ON THE WORLD SERIES VICTORY CELEBRATION . . .

We started at Disneyland and made our way back to the parking lot of Angel Stadium. There were 100,000 or 200,000 people, and to have all those people showing their support was pretty cool. It's probably the closest I will ever come to feeling like a rock star. Whenever I stepped onto the field, I would take into consideration the fact that I was playing for the fans. I never wanted to let them down. So it felt so good to be a part of that celebration with the fans, knowing we had won.

ON HIS PLAYING PHILOSOPHY . . .

The biggest thing I tried to do when I stepped on the field was to find a way to help the club win. Whatever that meant on any given day, I would put myself in a position to do it. I never worried about my stats and I never worried about anything other than finding a way to make myself valuable on the field.

ON JOINING THE ANGELS . . .

I was very fortunate to be on an American League club with a National League mind-set. Playing for Mike Scioscia allowed my career to blossom because I did not have to change anything about the way I played. The fans also took me under their wing. They were unbelievable in their support. I truly will never forget how special they are to me.

ON DARIN ERSTAD . . .

Ersty never really said much. I am a firm believer that actions speak louder than words, and in that sense he was a leader. He ran out every ball. He gave each play everything he had. He always had his mind in the game, and he expected the same attitude from every single one of his teammates. I definitely looked up to him and wanted to make sure I never let him down.

To reach the apex, the Angels had to get past the New York Yankees, winners of four of the last six world titles; the Central Division–champion Minnesota Twins; and eventually the National League champion, the San Francisco Giants, with baseball's newly crowned home run king, Barry Bonds.

In the first round, the Angels bombed the Bronx Bombers by scoring 31 runs, collecting 56 hits, hitting nine home runs, and batting .376 over four games.

The Yankees hit four home runs of their own in the opener to win, 8–5, in New York, but the Angels bats were hot for the next three games. They collected 17 hits and four homers (Troy Glaus, Tim Salmon, Garret Anderson, Scott Spiezio) in a Game 2 win, 8–6.

In Anaheim, the torrid hitting continued with 12 hits in Game 3 (homers by Salmon and Kennedy), a 9–6 victory, and 15 more hits (home run by Shawn Wooten) in the clincher, 9–5. Rookie Francisco Rodriguez won two games, and Troy Percival saved two.

Right The Angels could not be stopped on their way to the World Series.

Far Right Adam Kennedy tips his cap after hitting three home runs in the American League Championship Series against Minnesota.

It was on to Minnesota. Once again, the Angels lost the opener, this time 2–1, but went on to win the next four. Darin Erstad and Brad Fullmer homered in the second game, a 6–3 win, to even the series, and Jarrod Washburn and John Lackey both turned in strong pitching performances in the next two games to give the Angels a 3-1 lead.

Adam Kennedy, the second baseman from Northridge who had hit just seven homers during the regular season, then played Superman in Game 5. He homered in the third and again in the fifth, but the Angels trailed, 5–3, after six innings. In the seventh, with two on, Kennedy slammed his third homer of the game, a 3-run shot, to ignite a 10-run rally that catapulted the team to a 13–5 win and a berth in the World Series.

Rodriguez won two of the four games, and Percival had two more saves. Kennedy was the MVP.

In the seventh, with two on, Kennedy slammed his third homer of the game, a 3-run shot, to ignite a 10-run rally that catapulted the team to a 13–5 win and a berth in the World Series.

ON HIS BASES-LOADED DOUBLE IN GAME 7 OF THE 2002 WORLD SERIES . . .

In my first at bat, I hit a hard line drive to center field, I think off of a curveball. So my next time up, my approach was to look for a fastball, and fortunately I got one out over the plate, and you don't expect to get a pitch like that. I'm just happy I was able to do something with it and not hit it at somebody — rather, hit some outfield grass and let some runs score.

ON HIS 10-RBI GAME, AUGUST 21, 2007 . . .

Those kinds of things sneak up on you. We got out to a lead on the Yankees. We had been scoring and they had been scoring — it was one of those games that turned into a boat race. We were scoring a lot of runs, and eventually we just took off and dropped a bunch of runs on them. It kind of snuck up on me. When I hit the grand slam, I had already hit the three-run homer and had a couple doubles and drove in some runs — but when I hit the grand slam, running around the bases, that was a little different. I knew I had driven in a lot of runs that night, but during the game it was really hard for me to get really caught up in something individual like that.

ON CHONE FIGGINS . . .

He got here with his legs. He fought his way to get into the lineup, and he took advantage of that opportunity. The spark plug that he was at the top of the lineup enabled those of us in the middle of the lineup to do our job. He made our jobs easier by what he did on the bases, taking extra bases, stealing bases. You need to have that type of player on your team to be successful.

ON COACH ROD CAREW . . .

My personality would not let me get to the point where I got caught up in myself, and having a coach like Rod Carew kept me grounded as well. He pulled me aside and told me to focus on just playing every day. He showed me how to make sure I kept getting my work in, and he taught me not to worry about the stuff that would get written about me. He also taught me to be one of those players that work hard and keep their eyes focused on playing ball.

ON PLAYING WITH TIM SALMON AND JIM EDMONDS . . .

We were all hard workers, and we always made sure to get our work in. We knew we were confident players and we knew we had the ability to do some things, and we just went out there and played. We did not compete with each other. We were more concerned about making sure we established ourselves as everyday major leaguers.

ON MIKE SCIOSCIA . . .

His greatest asset was his attitude toward winning. It was unlike anything I had experienced before. He wanted us to take the extra base, to be more aggressive, and to not worry about making mistakes.

The Giants and Bonds awaited. The San Francisco slugger had hit a record 73 home runs the previous season and had won the fifth of his seven National League MVP awards in '02.

Most of the series was a slugfest. Bonds homered in each of the first three games and finished with four homers, two doubles, 13 walks, a .471 batting average, and an on-base percentage of .700.

But the Angels had more balance. Glaus, who was the MVP, hit .385 with three home runs. Salmon hit .346 with a pair of home runs, Eckstein .310, Erstad .300, and Anderson, Kennedy, and Bengie Molina were all at .280 or above. Despite Bonds' torrid start, the Angels took two of the first three games.

In the second game at Anaheim, the Angels and Giants were tied at 9–9 through seven innings. In the bottom of the eighth, Salmon hit his second homer of the game with Eckstein aboard for an 11–9 lead.

"I had faced [Felix] Rodriguez the night before and hit a line drive to right," said Salmon. "When I was in the on-deck circle, I knew he was coming with a fastball. I was very relaxed and swung easily. I knew immediately it was out. We knew there was going to be a hero in the dugout, and that night it was me.

"Then everything went through my mind in seconds, thinking about growing up as a kid and hitting a home run in the World Series, about Kirk Gibson running around the bases, about the 10 years of not making the playoffs. For me, it was the culmination of my career—all the emotions passed before me. It was a very introspective time.

"I think I made the most of my opportunities. It was awesome," Salmon said. "The way the game went back and forth was unbelievable."

Bonds homered with two outs in the ninth, but Percival got Benito Santiago to pop out to Kennedy for the final out in a 28-hit, 21-run game, 11–10.

In San Francisco, it was 57 degrees at game time, but the Angels bats didn't cool off. They collected 16 hits—three by Erstad—and rolled, 10–4. Spiezio had a two-run triple, and the bullpen was brilliant, with Brendan Donnelly and Scott Schoeneweis pitching four innings of one-hit relief.

Top David Eckstein's quickness and smarts enabled him to stand tall, even against the Giants' Barry Bonds.

Right Jose Molina waves a banner resurrecting the 1979 slogan.

Right Mike Scioscia greets Giants manager and former Dodgers teammate Dusty Baker to open the 2002 World Series.

Below World Series MVP Troy Glaus.

Bottom Right Angels fans stormed in the bleachers with their Thunder Stix, and the Rally Monkey jumped up and down on the jumbotron as everyone pulled for an Angels World Series victory.

"Then everything went through my mind in seconds, thinking about growing up as a kid and hitting a home run in the World Series, about Kirk Gibson running around the bases, about the 10 years of not making the playoffs. For me, it was the culmination of my career. All the emotions passed before me. It was a very introspective time."

Q&A with TIM SALMON

ON HIS FIRST MAJOR LEAGUE GAME . . .

Everything was spinning so fast, and then all of a sudden, the first inning started. I went up to the on-deck circle for my first at bat, and it was like the world stopped. I was in my comfort zone, and it was like, wow. I imagined myself being so nervous, and it was completely the opposite. It was so comforting because it was what I had been doing my whole life. When I got into the on-deck circle, I knew where I was.

ON THE TEAM CHEMISTRY IN 2002 . . .

It was a great chemistry; we all came together. We had some guys who were hungry, guys that really enjoyed hanging out together. It wasn't about clocking in and clocking out. A lot of guys were hanging out together away from the field, and then in the clubhouse it was very much a tone of "Hey, we've all got a job to do, and we need to make sure we are keeping everybody in check."

ON HIS SECOND HOME RUN IN GAME 2 OF THE WORLD SERIES . . .

I was running the bases, and the fans were just going bananas. There's nothing like that in the world. I've never been a "slow trot" guy, but I tried to slow that trot down. I slowed it down as much as I could and still it probably lasted five or six seconds. But in my mind it was about a half an hour. There was so much emotion. It was what I had been dreaming about, one of those moments that just catch you right where you are and you are like, "Wow, this is a dream come true, this is really happening."

ON THE COMEBACK IN GAME 6 OF THE WORLD SERIES . . .

We shouldn't have been surprised, because that had been our team all year long, the team that could come back from anything. We grinded it out until the last out, no matter what. You knew in the ninth inning we were going to come back and we were going to fight and scratch and claw. It was an amazing moment, and I'm so thankful we were able to turn it around.

ON TROY PERCIVAL . . .

Troy Percival is one of the greats. From a teammate's standpoint, a clubhouse has 25 different personalities, and you've got to have it all: You've got to have the quiet guys like me and you've got to have the guys like Percy who are going to be the rah-rah and fire you up and make sure the clubhouse is running smoothly. I'm so thankful we had him, for that reason.

ON GARRET ANDERSON . . .

Garret Anderson was as pure a hitter as they came. You knew you didn't mess with his swing: He knew how to hit the ball. He's an even-keel kind of guy, a great teammate and a great friend.

The Giants tied the series the next day when the Angels hit into three double plays. San Francisco scored the go-ahead run in the eighth for a 4–3 win despite another home run by Glaus.

The dark clouds of disaster descended on the Angels in Game 5 as the Giants scored four runs in both the seventh and eighth innings to crush the visitors, 16–4, and push them to within a game of elimination.

When San Francisco took a 5–0 lead into the seventh inning in Game 6, the 44,506 fans in Anaheim sat quietly, waiting for the clock to strike midnight.

The Angels, however, were about to get those fans on their feet. In the bottom of the seventh, Spiezio hit a three-run home run to make it 5–3. Erstad led off the eighth with a home run, and the deficit was but a run. Salmon and Anderson produced singles, and Glaus banged a double into left field for a 6–5 lead, and the collective crowd roared. Percival dispatched the Giants in order in the ninth, and the series was, once again, tied. After the thrilling comeback in Game 6, Game 7 was nearly anti-climatic. Scioscia started rookie John Lackey, and

he proved solid for five innings. Anderson gave the Angels pitchers all they would need when he lined a bases-loaded double, his lone extra-base hit in the series, down the right field line in the bottom of the third to score all three runners and give the Angels a 4–1 lead. Donnelly, Rodriguez, and Percival took over for Lackey and allowed just two hits while striking out six in the final four innings.

Kenny Lofton was the last batter for San Francisco. He hit a fly ball to center field.

It was just a routine fly ball. One of tens of thousands that had been hit over 42 seasons in Anaheim. It floated lazily into the night sky and settled softy into the glove of the Erstad, who remembered that his dad always said to "use both hands." An explosion erupted throughout the stadium.

The final out of the 2002 World Series had been recorded, and the Angels were, for the very first time, champions of the world.

The celebration ran from the Pacific Ocean to Disneyland, from the far reaches of the San Fernando Valley to the deserts of Palm Springs. The Angels were the champions of the world. Forty-two years of frustration had ended.

Left Jarrod Washburn left everything on the field.

Below The Angels prepare to take on the Giants in San Francisco.

Yes we did: The Angels celebrate their first World Series Championship.

Braintrust: Bobby Ramos, Mike Scioscia, Alfredo Griffin, Joe Maddon, Mickey Hatcher, Ron Roenicke, and Bud Black celebrate in the managers' office.

The echoes of Gene Autry and Bill Rigney and Gene Mauch resounded through the Stadium. Angels everywhere rejoiced.

BOBBY WINKLES: "I was watching the games at home in La Quinta and was very, very happy for them, but the biggest sorrow was that Mr. Autry wasn't alive. He deserved to be there."

DICK ENBERG, in his autobiography, *Oh My!*: "I was on an airplane when the pilot came on and announced the Angels had won the world championship. When he said that, I was jolted by my reaction. Although I had not been associated with the team for many years, I burst into tears. I couldn't believe how much I still cared."

ROD CAREW: "I was home. I always have rooted for the team and was thrilled that they won one at last."

JIM FREGOSI: "I felt terrible that Gene [Autry] was not there, but it was wonderful for the organization that I grew up in. I made it to several games in Anaheim, and it was certainly outstanding."

BOBBY GRICH: "I really believe the fans had a lot to do with that team winning it all in 2002. It was the first year the team had gone to the all-red uniforms, and the fans started wearing a lot of red to the games. I had just gone back to work for the team, and it was great to be a part of it."

CLYDE WRIGHT: "I was in one of those field-level suites, and it was just like I was still playing. I got goose bumps and all."

"For all the Angels fans who have been here from the beginning, and all the Angels we had above, this championship is for you," Scioscia told the crowd.

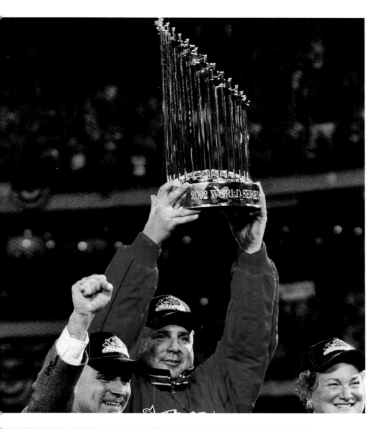

Left Mike Scioscia, flanked by general manager Bill Stoneman and Jackie Autry, lifts up the World Series Trophy for all to see.

Below Left Commissioner Bud Selig presents Disney president Michael Eisner with the World Series trophy.

Two days later, the party was at Disneyland, where a parade was held for the World Champions, followed by a rally at the stadium. City officials estimated more than 100,000 people were in attendance at the two events. "For all the Angels fans who have been here from the beginning, and all the Angels we had above, this championship is for you," Scioscia told the crowd. "I waited 10 years for something like this," said Salmon. "But I know you guys have been waiting a lot longer. This is yours."

That same year had been the first time the Angels had changed their colors to all red, and the players felt the difference. "Sometimes, you never knew who your fans were," recalled Salmon. "But that year, you saw all our fans in red, and you knew they were rooting for you. It was very cool and still is. I was cognizant that the win meant a lot to a lot of people both inside the organization and outside. It's like we had come full circle."

"I've been in this game for a long time and have never been around a group of guys so passionate," Scioscia said. "I think our whole team stepped up and did what we had to do. For me to look at the past, the Angels, they've had championships here. They've won divisions. They've never gotten to the level we have. For us to get to this level is very, very rewarding."

Some days are better than others, but there is only one best day. For the Angels and their fans, it was October 27, 2002. After 42 years, they had won the right to call themselves World Champions.

Right The World Series celebration parade rolls through the Angel Stadium parking lot.

MAY 15, 2003
ARTE MORENO BECOMES NEW ANGELS OWNER

★★★

Arturo "Arte" Moreno became the third owner of the Angels when he purchased the team from the Walt Disney Corporation for $182.5 million.

The sale of the team was approved unanimously by major league owners. "This sale went through the ownership committee, executive council, and ownership as fast as anything I've ever seen in all my years in baseball," Commissioner Bud Selig said at a news conference. "[Moreno is] what you hope you're going to get when you get an owner."

Moreno is a Vietnam veteran and a graduate of the University of Arizona. He was the president and CEO of Outdoor Systems before it was sold in 1998.

Moreno, along with 17 other investors including actor Bill Murray, was part of an ownership group of the Salt Lake City Trappers minor league baseball team. Moreno was also a minority owner in both the Arizona Diamondbacks and the Phoenix Suns.

A year later, a new and exciting era, one that proved to be the most successful in history, dawned. In May of 2003, Arte Moreno, a highly successful and much-respected businessman from Arizona, bought the Angels and became the third team owner after Gene Autry and the Walt Disney Company.

The oldest of 11 children, the Tucson native and lifelong baseball fan brought fresh ideas and boundless enthusiasm to the game. "I guess I look at baseball as something that historically has been here for a long time," Moreno said. "It's a fun thing. It's a kids' game. I think long-term, the balance of entertainment will always lean toward baseball. I think it's just part of our culture."

He cut ticket, souvenir, and concession prices, frequently visited fans in the stands during games, and two years later expanded the franchise's fan base by renaming the team the Los Angeles Angels of Anaheim. In 2003, the team drew over 3 million fans for the first time, and by 2006, the franchise's value had more than doubled. "The fans own the team—I'm the economic caretaker," he said. The Angels would surpass the 3 million attendance figure every year for the rest of the decade.

After injuries to Erstad and Glaus derailed the 2003 team, owner Arte Moreno signed free-agent Vladimir Guerrero (for $70 million over five years) in the off-season. He would, over the next six seasons, become the Angels' most prolific offensive threat. In his first year, he hit 39 home runs, drove in 126, scored a league-best 124 times, stole 15 of 18 bases, and was an overwhelming choice as the league's Most Valuable Player, garnering 21 of 28 votes.

Guerrero was a brute at the plate, slashing and bashing away, taking balls out of the strike zone and rifling them to all parts of the field. He played with a boyish enthusiasm and quickly proved to be one of the most popular players in franchise history.

Guerrero averaged 29 home runs, 103 RBI, and a batting average of .319 (highest in team history) during his Anaheim days, making the All-Star team four times and winning the All-Star Home Run Derby in 2007.

> "It's a fun thing. It's a kids' game. I think long-term, the balance of entertainment will always lean toward baseball. I think it's just part of our culture."

Above Vladimir Guerrero earned MVP honors in 2004.

JULY 14–15, 2003
GARRET ANDERSON SHINES AS AN ALL-STAR

U.S. Cellular Field, Chicago

★★

The best player in baseball for two nights in July of 2003 was the Angels' Garret Anderson.

Exhibiting highlight performances on consecutive nights, the Angels left fielder stole the show at the annual All-Star festivities in Chicago.

On Monday, Anderson won the Home Run Derby by outhitting the Cardinals' young slugger Albert Pujols.

The following evening, he delivered a home run, a double, and a single to lead the American League to a dramatic 7–6 come-from-behind win.

The AL had trailed by four runs, 5–1, entering the sixth inning when Anderson hit a two-run home run off Woody Williams. In the bottom half of the eighth, Anderson's one-out double off the Dodgers' Eric Gagne (who did not blow a save all season except in the All-Star Game), was his third hit of the night and started a three-run rally capped by Hank Blalock's game-winning two-run home run.

The AL win, 7–6, saw Angels reliever Brendan Donnelly as the winning pitcher, Mike Scioscia the winning manager, and Anderson named the game's MVP, his second trophy in as many nights.

With Guerrero's arrival in 2004 and Moreno's willingness to allow his general managers, Bill Stoneman and then Tony Reagins, to acquire top free agents, the Angels began an unprecedented run, winning the American League West title five times over the next six years. Stoneman, who pitched two no-hitters in the majors with the Montreal Expos, was the most successful and longest-tenured general manager in the franchise's first 50 years. During his eight seasons, the Angels made it to the playoffs four times and posted a winning percentage of .542 (703-593).

An eighth-inning rally in Oakland in early October of '04 gave the Angels a 5-4 win and clinched the West in a game that saw Guerrero hit his 39th homer of the season. It was their first division title in 18 seasons. The Angels led the league in hitting (.282) and stolen bases (143).

In the American League Championship Series, the team was swept by the Boston Red Sox in three straight as the Angels pitchers yielded 25 runs in the series and the offense managed to hit only .226. Curt Schilling and Pedro Martinez pitched for the Red Sox in Anaheim and catapulted Boston to a 2-0 game lead. The Angels did not go down without a fight in Game 3 in Fenway. Down 6–1 in the 7th inning, they scored a run on a bases-loaded walk, and then Guerrero unloaded a grand slam home run to tie it. Boston, though, closed out the series when David Ortiz hit a two-run homer in the bottom of the 10th.

Above Vladimir Guerrero displays his MVP trophy at the BBWAA dinner in New York.

Right UCLA product Troy Glaus was a local favorite.

JUNE 2, 2004
VLADDY'S BIG NIGHT

The "Big A"

★★★

Vladimir Guerrero, who would be named the Most Valuable Player in the American League for 2004, had one of the more remarkable and memorable games in the history of the Angels, if not in all of baseball, on June 2.

Against Boston Red Sox ace Pedro Martinez, Guerrero homered in the first inning with a man aboard and slugged a two-run double in the third to score Chone Figgins and David Eckstein. In the fourth, he hit a sacrifice fly for another RBI and then slugged another home run, a three-run shot, in the sixth off Mike Timlin. In the seventh inning, Guerrero capped his offensive display with an RBI single.

The Angels won the game, 10–7, as a crowd of 43,205 watched Guerrero drive in nine runs. Eckstein also had a huge night, collecting five hits and scoring four times.

ON HITTING PITCHES OFF THE GROUND . . .

Sometimes it's just an accident. I start to swing, and then I can't stop and then I hit the ball off the ground. It always made me laugh because my teammates would always ask, "How did you hit that ball?" And I don't know how I did it. Sometimes I just couldn't stop my swing.

ON NOT WEARING BATTING GLOVES . . .

As a young boy I would work with my hands. Some people would wear [gloves], but I never did. I always grabbed the bat with my bare hands. I also would always dirty my helmet and my hands to give me a better grip on the bat.

ON HIS 2004 MVP SEASON . . .

At the beginning of the season, I was not doing well. My knees were hurting. Eventually, they started to get better and I started to get used to the pitching again. And then, thank God, I began to hit the ball and have a great season.

They told me I was going to win the MVP, but I did not think so, because there were so many other players who had played well that year. But they called me after a game and told me I won. So I took a bath and went to the owner's suite to celebrate.

ON HIS HIT IN THE NINTH INNING AGAINST BOSTON IN THE 2009 PLAYOFFS . . .

At first I thought I would not swing. But then I thought, "I'm going to swing." And I hit the ball to center field.

ON MIKE SCIOSCIA . . .

He let us play, and he did not put pressure on us. I liked playing for a manager like that.

OCTOBER 2, 2004
ANGELS RALLY FOR AL WEST CROWN

Oakland–Alameda County Coliseum, Oakland

★★

The Angels needed to win two games in the final series of the season against the A's to win their first pennant in 18 years.

Seldom-used Alfredo Amezaga hit a grand slam home run in the sixth inning of the first game to help the Angels to an easy 10–0 win on Friday.

Oakland featured their ace, Barry Zito, in the Saturday contest. A home run by Vladimir Guerrero tied the score at 2–2 in the sixth, but the A's took a 4–2 lead in the bottom of the inning.

Bengie Molina led off the eighth with a single, and Chone Figgins singled to center with one out. Darin Erstad then drove a pitch deep into right field for a two-run double to tie the game. Troy Glaus flew out for the second out of the inning, but Garret Anderson forged a slow roller through the infield, and Erstad scored to give the Angels a 5–4 lead.

Relievers Francisco Rodriguez and Troy Percival pitched the final two innings to give the Angels the win and the American League West Championship.

Below Angels celebrate a win over Oakland that clinched the Western Division title in 2004.

Right Moreno welcomes Bartolo Colon, another free agent acquisition and future Cy Young Award winner.

Bartolo Colon, who had been signed prior to the '04 season, won the Cy Young Award in 2005, going 21-8 as the Angels won the West again, this time by 7 games over the A's.

Chone Figgins, playing six different positions throughout the year, led the league in stolen bases with 62 and scored 113 runs.

In the postseason, the Angels advanced one step further, defeating the Yankees in the American League Championship Series before running into the Chicago White Sox.

Catcher Bengie Molina homered three times against New York, and Garret Anderson hit two more. The Angels won the fifth and deciding game in Anaheim, 5–3, as four Angels pitchers stranded 11 Yankees, Anderson hit a two-run shot, and Adam Kennedy added a two-run triple. Molina hit .444 against the Yankees, Juan Rivera .353, and Guerrero .333.

Their opponent in the AL Championship Series was the White Sox. The Angels won the opener in Chicago, 3–2, thanks, in part, to a home run by Anderson, but Chicago won Game 2 and then swept the Halos in Anaheim when the host team could manage but 15 hits in three games to finish the series with a batting average of .175.

After a non-pennant-winning '06, the Angels ran off three straight titles.

Scioscia proved to have a magician's touch in shaping his roster each year. He integrated speed in the form of Figgins, who stole 280 bases from 2002 to 2009. He blended young players like Howie Kendrick, Mike Napoli, Jered Weaver, and Joe Saunders with veterans. Guerrero continued to carry the offense, but the supporting cast was always evolving around him. Francisco Rodriguez, the high-kicking Venezuelan with a violent delivery, took over the closer role in 2005 and saved a remarkable 194 games, including a major-league-record 62 in '08, over the next four years.

1995–2004

PERCIVAL SETS CLUB SAVES RECORD

The "Big A"

★★★

Troy Percival saved 316 games over his 10-year Angels career, the most in club history.

Over a nine-year span, "Percy" had 27 or more saves each season with a high of 42 in 1998. A four-time All-Star, Percival never led the league in

saves but finished in the top 10 nine times and the top 5 six times.

Percival pitched in 579 games for the Angels, all in relief.

Q&A with TROY PERCIVAL

ON COACH ROD CAREW . . .

He was really tough on me, and there was a reason for it: He knew the team was counting on me, and he was testing my merit, and I guess I passed muster. There's nobody who knows more about reading hitters than he does. We would sit together in the dugout during batting practice. He would start picking out points on hitters, telling me to watch this guy's hands and how his grip shows he can't hit this pitch. He taught me how to read hitters, and I used what I learned from him for my whole career.

ON CHUCK FINLEY . . .

Chuck Finley was the toughest guy you'll ever see take the mound. He would go out there and give up four runs in the first inning, and he'd still be out there in the eighth inning after 140 pitches, not willing to give the ball up. This guy just didn't want to come out of the game, and I think anybody who has ever talked about Chuck Finley will have nothing but respect for the fact that he never wanted to come off the mound.

ON THE 2002 AL DIVISION SERIES VERSUS THE YANKEES . . .

We expected to win every game by the time we got to the playoffs, which seems kind of weird for a team that's never been there. But I remember standing on the line during the national anthem and looking down the line at our guys, looking for fear in their faces and there was none. That team had no fear.

ON SWITCHING FROM CATCHER TO PITCHER . . .

I think when they drafted me, they probably had it in the back of their heads that I was not going to end up as a catcher. I had a coach named Bob Clear who did not hold any punches when it came to telling me about switching positions. He would tell me I was the worst hitter this organization has ever seen. He told me I had to get on the mound and pitch. I finally did it, and then our pitching coaches basically taught me how to pitch. They knew I had the mentality, and they taught me the technique. I took off my catcher's gear and they molded me into the pitcher they wanted. They let me be aggressive and they fine-tuned my mechanics so that I could pitch a little bit longer. I loved every minute of it.

ON MIKE SCIOSCIA . . .

He always held preworkout meetings during Spring Training. He was really funny and had a great sense of humor. He would start getting on the rookies, and he could make everybody laugh. But when it came time to work, he made sure we knew it was time to work. We were pushed every day in Spring Training, and we worked harder than other teams. I believe to this day that we won the World Series because of how we worked during the spring under Mike Scioscia.

NOVEMBER 8, 2005

COLON WINS THE CY YOUNG

★★

Angels ace Bartolo Colon, the barrel-chested right-hander from the Dominican Republic, was awarded the 2005 Cy Young Award for his outstanding season-long performance that resulted in a glittering 21-8 record.

Colon became the second Angel—and the first in 41 years—to win the Cy Young. (The first was Dean Chance in 1964.)

Colon finished in the top 10 in virtually every statistical category: first in wins with 21, eighth in ERA at 3.48, seventh in innings pitched with 222.2, and eighth in strikeouts with 157.

Colon easily outdistanced the competition in the voting, receiving 17 first-place votes to just 8 for runner-up Mariano Rivera of the Yankees and 3 for Johan Santana of the Twins.

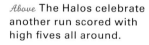

In 2007, the Angels proved solid from opening day on. They won 13 of 19 late in the season and by mid-September had a 9½-game lead in the West. Guerrero drove in 125 runs, and Figgins hit .330, with 41 steals and 43 extra-base hits. John Lackey had a breakout year, too, winning 19 and leading the league in ERA with a 3.01 mark.

On a warm night in August of that season, Garret Anderson had what amounted to a good week—perhaps a month—inside a few innings against the Yankees in Anaheim. The quiet left fielder cracked a pair of doubles that drove in three runs in his first two times at the plate and followed that with two home runs, one with two on and one with the bases loaded. His final stat line looked like one from a video game: four hits, two doubles, two home runs, and a club-record 10 RBI.

But the lack of hitting was the culprit in the playoffs when the Red Sox won three in a row in the division championship. The Angels failed to homer and managed a .192 average over the series.

Above Francisco Rodriguez and Jeff Mathis revel in victory as the Angels clinch the Western Division in 2007. Mike Napoli joins the merriment as the rest of the team rushes in.

Right Vladimir Guerrero celebrates with Arte Moreno after the Angels clinch the AL West in 2007.

Q&A with CHONE FIGGINS

ON PINCH-RUNNING FOR THE ANGELS IN 2002 . . .

I did a lot of running in the tunnel to warm up. Just staying loose and hitting in the cages, playing catch. I knew the situation because we were chasing the wild card, and I knew if it was a close ballgame in the sixth or seventh inning, I had a chance to come in and pinch run.

ON THE WORLD SERIES CELEBRATION . . .

It happened so fast. You could see the ball going in the air to Erstad, and it was in slow motion and everybody was kind of on the field before he caught the ball, and then we all stormed the field.

ON DARIN ERSTAD . . .

He loved to play the game. He would put everything out there that he could. He would break every bone in his body to get an out on defense or break up a double play if he was running the bases.

ON BEING NAMED 2005 TEAM CO-MVP . . .

To be voted MVP by my teammates was huge. They get to see me play every day, and the fact that they recognized me as a factor in winning the division is special. To have the honor to be able to represent my team like that is very important.

ON HITTING FOR THE CYCLE IN 2006 . . .

It is tough to do. Usually it's the power guys hitting home runs. For me, home runs are rare. And then the triple, that is almost tougher than hitting a home run. Hitting a double and a single are tough, too, because unless it's a hustle double, I am going to third anyway.

ON HIS SIX-HIT GAME JUNE 18, 2007. . .

I did not even realize I had six hits because the game was so close. We kept fighting back to stay in it. The Astros were beating us early, and we had to fight to even tie the game. When I hit, I did not know anything special was going on until people started telling me. I was just excited that we ended up winning the game.

ON DAVID ECKSTEIN . . .

He is the kind of player you want your kids to look up to. People always said he could not do this, he could not do that. But you see how successfully he played, and it's a good lesson to kids that no matter how good you are, you have to keep pushing and going forward no matter what people say about you. David is very intelligent. He understands what is important to the team.

The 2008 Angels are the first and only Angels team to win 100 games in a season, going 100-62. They rode into first place on May 14 and stayed there all summer, going 35-16 in June and July. They won the West by a whopping 21 games. They won 50 games at home, 50 games away.

It was a remarkable team in that the offense did not produce anyone who hit 30 homers or drive in 100 runs. All five starting pitchers recorded double-digit wins, and Rodriguez posted his record 62 saves. They won in every fashion imaginable, with a clutch hit one night, a sparkling defensive play the next, and a stout bullpen effort the next.

In a bold midsummer move, general manager Tony Reagins shipped Casey Kotchman to Atlanta for switch-hitting slugger Mark Teixeira, who helped a good offense become even better. In 54 games, Teixeira hit .358 with 13 home runs and 43 RBI. He would be just as good in the playoffs.

Armed and healthy, the Angels approached the postseason with a resolute confidence. But Boston stood in their way once more. The Angels lost two close games in Anaheim before the trip to the East Coast. Mike Napoli homered twice in Game 3, and the Angels were back in the series with a 5–4 win. Boston, however, closed it out with another close victory, 3–2, in the fourth game.

Guerrero (.467), Teixeira (.467), Torii Hunter (.389), and Figgins (.333) all had solid playoff averages.

Below. Francisco Rodriguez set the new record for saves in a single season when he posted 62 in 2008.

Above. Torii Hunter brought his outstanding brand of defense to the Angels outfield in 2008.

Below. Mike Napoli and teammates jump for joy after a walk-off win on September 12, 2008.

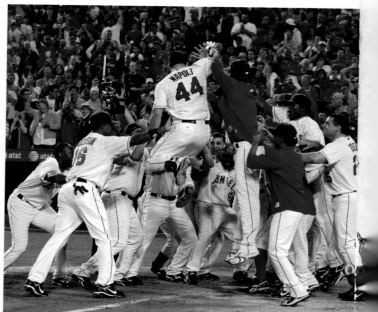

JUNE 18, 2007
FIGGINS COLLECTS SIX HITS

Angel Stadium

★★★

Chone Figgins spent all but the last day of April on the disabled list, batted .156 in May, and finished the first half of the season in an 0-for-21 slump.

But from May 31 through September 22, Figgins batted .403, a span of 83 games where the speedy leadoff man reached base in 46 percent of his plate appearances. Despite his early and late woes, Figgins finished with a .330 batting average, the seventh highest in Angels' history.

On the night of June 18, Figgins had his brightest moment of the season, going 6 for 6 and leading the Angels to a 10–9 comeback victory over the Houston Astros at Angel Stadium.

Figgins's final hit was a ninth-inning walk-off triple down the right field line, scoring Reggie Willits from first base to complete the Angels' comeback.

Figgins's six hits tied Garret Anderson's team record, set in 1996.

A bird's-eye view of Angel Stadium circa 2007.

Mike Scioscia congratulates Francisco Rodriquez after the pitcher recorded his 62nd save of the season.

Torii Hunter swims in the success of a championship season.

Q&A with SCOT SHIELDS

ON THE MENTALITY OF A SETUP MAN . . .

When you are on the mound: no fear. You need to go out there and throw strikes and make them hit the ball. One of the biggest things is to forget what happened the day before, whether good or bad. That helped me out a lot: to go out and just think about the task at hand.

ON THE GRITTIEST ANGELS . . .

Darin Erstad: the way he played the game, he played it all-out, anything goes. He really did not worry about his body when he was out there playing the field. He has to top the list, but you can go down the list to Adam Kennedy, Scott Spiezio, David Eckstein. Take your pick, and they are all gamers.

ON THE ANGELS FANS . . .

The fans at Angel Stadium are really loud; it was really fun to go to work there every day. The atmosphere is such a great place. Those thundersticks, they get loud, and the fans get loud. There's no better place to play. When the fans got loud and got crazy, that really helped us get going.

ON MIKE SCIOSCIA . . .

Mike Scioscia knows how to deal with people on a personal, individual basis. He lets you play the game, lets you have fun, but when it's time to get down to business, it's time to go. You played hard, and that is Angels baseball: First to third, we play aggressive. That all came from him.

ON THE 2002 TEAM'S SUCCESS . . .

We played Angels baseball. We did all the small things, we took extra bases. We had a lot of power, we hit a lot of home runs, but I think it was just the aggressive play, and no matter how much we were down late in the game, we never gave up, we always battled back, and we always put together big innings.

SEPTEMBER 13, 2008
K-ROD BECOMES SINGLE-SEASON SAVES LEADER

The "Big A"

★★★

Angels closer Francisco Rodriguez became base-ball's all-time single-season saves leader when he recorded his 58th against the Seattle Mariners in a 5–2 win that extended the Angels' lead in the American League West to 18 1/2 games over Texas.

Rodriguez entered the game in the top of the ninth and immediately found himself in trouble as Miguel Cairo doubled and Luis Valbuena walked. But K-Rod got the dangerous Ichiro Suzuki to ground out and then struck out Wladimir Balentien and Raul Ibanez for his 58th save, one more than Bobby Thigpen of

the Chicago White Sox, who held the record for 18 years.

Rodriguez would go on to save 62 games for the season.

Angels closers have saved 40 or more games seven other times: Bryan Harvey (46 in 1991), Troy Percival (42 in 1998 and 40 in 2002), Rodriguez (45 in 2005, 47 in 2006, and 40 in 2007), and Brian Fuentes (48 in 2009).

Scioscia kept the team on the beam in '09, winning another American League West title. Two newcomers to the lineup made up for the loss of Teixeira, who signed a free-agent contract with the Yankees in the off-season. Kendrys Morales, a flashy first baseman from Cuba, became a full-fledged power hitter with 34 home runs, 108 RBI, and a .306 batting average. Bobby Abreu, a highly respected veteran outfielder from Venezuela, joined the lineup and drove in 103 runs while teaching teammates to exhibit more patience at the plate.

The Angels had brought in another quality free agent in 2008, signing center fielder Torii Hunter from the Minnesota Twins. Hunter, gregarious as he was gifted, became an immediate hit in the locker room and on the field. A tremendous defender, he arrived with seven Gold Gloves and added two more in '08 and '09. He shouldered his share of the offense and by 2010 was the cleanup hitter.

The 2009 season began with a tragedy when promising young pitcher Nick Adenhart was killed in a late-night car accident after pitching five shutout innings earlier in the evening. The Angels paid tribute to the 22-year-old Adenhart throughout the season, and when they clinched the division title they poured champagne and beer on one of his jerseys.

Left Teammates Erick Aybar and Bobby Abreu.

Left Chone Figgins and Torii Hunter in a pregame ritual.

Below Vladimir Guerrero comes home after a walk-off homerun.

The Angels finally got past the Red Sox in '09 by sweeping Boston in three straight. Lackey and Weaver were tough at home in 5–0 and 4–1 respective wins, and then the Angels pulled off one of their touchstone rallies in Fenway in Game 3. Juan Rivera delivered a two-run single in the eighth and Abreu a run-scoring double in the ninth, and Guerrero gave them the lead and the win with a smashing single up the middle to score two more and give the Halos a 6–5 lead and the sweep.

The Yankees were up next, a team the Angels had much success against in recent years.

After CC Sabathia held the Angels to four hits in the opener, a 4–1 Yankees win, three of the next four games were decided by a single run.

In Game 2 in New York, Figgins drove in the go-ahead run in the top of the 11th, but Alex Rodriguez tied it with a home run in the bottom of the inning, and the Yankees won it in the 13th on a throwing error by the usually reliable Maicer Izturis. New York was up by two games.

Game 3 went extra innings, too, with Jeff Mathis doubling home Howie Kendrick for a 5–4 win despite four New York homers.

Sabathia came back to throttle the Angels once again, winning Game 4 on a five-hitter, 10–1.

The Angels continued to exhibit grit when they hung on in Game 5, 7–6, with Abreu, Guerrero, and Morales driving in runs in a three-run seventh.

The Yankees closed it out in New York in Game 6, 5–2.

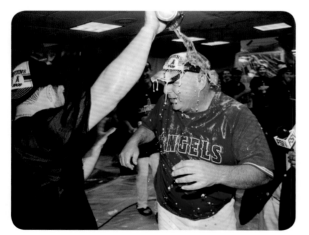

Left After guiding the Angels to their fifth division title in six years, Mike Scioscia gets a champagne shower.

Right Jered Weaver and teammates watch their playoff hopes soar as they defeat the Texas Rangers 11–0 with 17 games left to play in the 2009 season.

AUGUST 18, 2009
NINE FOR NINE

Jacobs Field, Cleveland

★★

A rare feat was accomplished late in the 2009 season when the Angels boasted every player in their lineup carrying a .300 batting average or better. At the conclusion of the 117th game of the season, the nine Angels in the lineup (with their averages) against Cleveland were Chone Figgins (.308), Bobby Abreu (.310), Juan Rivera (.310), Vladimir Guerrero (.313), Kendry Morales (.303), Torii Hunter (.307), Maicer Izturis (.300), Mike Napoli (.300), and Erick Aybar (.313)

Only Morales (.306), Izturis (.300), and Aybar (.312) would finish the year with averages at .300 or better, but five other players hit over .290 (Hunter, .299; Figgins, .298; Guerrero, .295; Abreu, .293; and Howie Kendrick, .291). The team batting average of .285 was best in club history.

It marked the first time since 1934 that a major league team at least 100 games into a season finished a game with every player in its starting lineup hitting .300 or better.

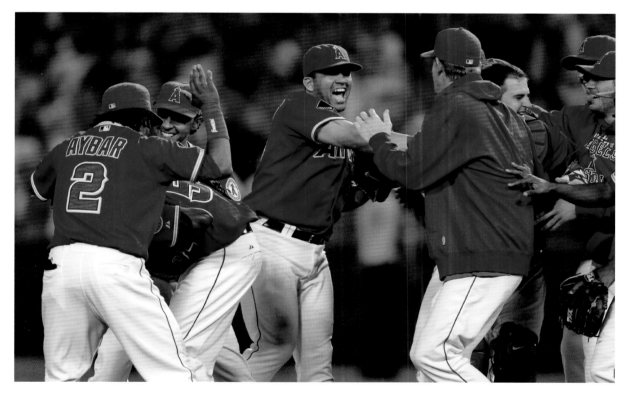

These Pages Ervin Santana is mobbed by teammates after his shutout performance helps clinch the 2009 American League Western Division title.

ON THE MENTALITY OF WORLD SERIES CHAMPIONS . . .

Our focus all along was to take it one step at a time. When you saw guys like Troy Percival and Garret Anderson and Tim Salmon first make the playoffs after being so close in the '90s with some great Angels teams, you felt good with that accomplishment, but we understood that the playoffs were only the first rung of a ladder. We knew we could reach the top of the ladder, and we always kept that in perspective. We made sure that our guys felt the momentum and understood, "Look, we can reach the top; we can not only get to the World Series but we can be world champions." They understood it, and they weren't going to be satisfied with just making the playoffs or just getting to the World Series.

ON THE LAST OUT OF THE 2002 WORLD SERIES . . .

It could not have been scripted any better. Darin Erstad, the guy who left body parts on that field all year long—for him to catch the last out of the first World Championship of this organization was incredible. When I saw Ersty spreading his arms and saying, "I got it!". . . what a feeling.

ON TIM SALMON . . .

Tim Salmon was an incredible player, an incredible talent, an incredible person, and he had an incredible impact on our organization. Even in the years that it was tough, he came out here every day with a focus that was uncanny, almost too focused. There could be a train wreck next to him, and he would not even sense it on the field because he was focused and had that tunnel vision that an elite player needs to have.

ON DAVID ECKSTEIN . . .

Really, he was a second baseman, and Alfredo Griffin, our third base coach, convinced me that this guy can play shortstop at a time that we desperately needed a shortstop. As he grew into that position, it became very apparent that he was going to play shortstop at a level that we needed for us to have a chance to reach our goals. As the season went on, he got better and better, and he was as good a leadoff hitter as you are ever going to see in baseball.

ON VLADIMIR GUERRERO . . .

Vladimir Guerrero is the most unassuming superstar you are ever going to find. He just loves to play baseball, he is great with teammates, great in the clubhouse. He is absolutely a player that has the most bat speed and the best ability to square up a baseball that I have seen in all my years in the game. I think he would rival anybody who has ever put on the uniform and stepped into a batter's box.

In 2010, the Angels hosted the Midsummer Classic for the third time. With 45,408 in attendance, it brought the total for the three games to 154,753. This time, it was the National League winning, for the first time in 13 years, 3–1.

Hunter made the All-Star team for the second time as an Angel, and Weaver was chosen for the first time. Weaver became the 61st individual Angel in the first 50 years to represent the team in the annual All-Star Game.

As the celebration of 50 Angels seasons unfolded in 2011, it remained clear that the team was continuing to maintain its place as one of the premier franchises in Major League Baseball.

And—fitting for the occasion—it was a season of past, present, and future: Former players were honored before every home game as part of the festivities, the team was competitive in navigating its way through the American League West, and a bevy of young players energized fans with both excitement and hope.

All the ingredients necessary for elite status were firmly in place:

★ Attendance was again near the top of the American League, with almost 40,000 fans packing into the Big A on a daily basis.

★ Young players from the farm system established themselves as major contributors on the big league roster, a fact that bodes well for the future.

★ The team was contending for a playoff spot until the last week of the season as the combination of youth and experience enabled manager Mike Scioscia to turn his magic into wins. On May 8, 2011, the highly respected skipper registered his 1,000th career win, becoming only the 56th man in history to reach that milestone and only the 23rd with one team.

★ Another hometown hero who emerged as one of the game's brightest stars was Long Beach State alum Jered Weaver, who opened the season with six consecutive wins and carried an ERA under 2.00 into the second half of the season. With that spectacular first few months of the season on his resume, Weaver was selected to his second straight All-Star team and was the American League's starting pitcher. Weaver signed a five-year contract extension on August 23.

★ And, of course, a salute to Angels history as alumnus player after alumnus player was introduced to the home crowd before throwing out the ceremonial first pitch. From Eli Grba, the opening-game pitcher in 1961, to Albie Pearson, from Dean Chance to Bob Rodgers, from Nolan Ryan to Bobby Grich and Jim Abbott, the ex-Angels paraded to the center of the diamond amid cheers of appreciation from the loyal fans.

Above Torii Hunter earns his "Spider-Man" nickname.

Right Former teammates Alfredo Griffin, Fernando Valenzuela, Mickey Hatcher, and Mike Scioscia reunite before a 2011 game at Angel Stadium.

As Scioscia managed the team for the 12th season, he skillfully integrated young with old, speed with power, pitching with defense.

Weaver, blossoming into one of the dominant pitchers in the American League, was backed by the hardworking, always reliable veteran Dan Haren, who gave the club quality start after quality start. Ervin Santana and Joel Pineiro, who entered the season with 173 combined major league victories, gave the team two more solid starters, and rookie Tyler Chatwood, from nearby Yucaipa, often pitched with savvy that belied his years.

Twenty-one-year-old Chatwood was one of a handful of rookies and first-year players that lit up the stadium throughout the spring and summer. Joining him were Mark Trumbo, 25, Hank Conger, 23, Peter Bourjos, 24, Jordan Walden, 23, and 19-year-old Mike Trout, all originally drafted by the Angels and a further tribute to the organization.

Like Chatwood, both first baseman Mark Trumbo and catcher Hank Conger were local products, following in a long Angels tradition of culling players from surrounding high schools, like Andy Messersmith (Western High, Anaheim), Brian Downing (Magnolia High, Anaheim), Mike Witt (Servite High, Anaheim), Jim Edmonds (Diamond Bar High, Diamond Bar), Troy Percival (Moreno Valley High, Moreno Valley), and Garret Anderson (Kennedy High, Granada Hills). Trumbo, a six-four power hitter from Villa Park High, led the Pacific Coast League in home runs in 2010 and then led the Angels in home runs in 2011, while Huntington Beach High's Conger, the MVP of the 2010 All-Star Futures Game, began logging significant time

behind the plate while polishing a powerful swing.

Centerfielder Peter Bourjos, who had stolen 50 bases in one minor league season and twice led his league in triples, spent the second half of 2010 with the Angels and further exhibited his roadrunner speed on the outfield in 2011. Closer Jordan Walden showcased a 100-mile-per-hour fastball out of the bullpen.

The Angels could also boast of the No. 1 prospect in all of baseball in speedy and powerful outfielder Mike Trout. In his first two and a half seasons in the minors, Trout averaged .341 with 95 stolen bases and 93 extra base hits. Trout got his first taste of the majors when he was called up from AA in early July. At 19 years, 335 days, Trout became the youngest player to make his big league debut for the Angels

Above Chuck Finley shares a moment with Tyler Chatwood before tossing out a ceremonial first pitch.

Below Jordan Walden hit 100 on the radar gun and appeared in the All-Star Game.

Top Huntington Beach's Hank Conger is the Angels' catcher of the future.

Above Peter Bourjos displays Gold Glove–caliber defensive skills in center field.

since May 30, 1971, when pitcher Andy Hassler debuted at age 19 years, 224 days.

Said Trumbo about the newest Angels, "We all know what we need to do. I think we all play very similar styles, we have a lot of passion for it, and we have our priorities in line. I think that's only going to help us later on."

The young players were all playing second fiddle, though, to the veterans led by 28-year-old Weaver, the six-seven right-hander who has been part of the rotation since 2006, when he burst onto the scene with an 11-2 record. Scioscia has seen him dramatically elevate his game over the seasons.

"He's not intimidated by any situation," Scioscia said. "He understands his stuff better as he's gotten older. He's gotten to a point where he knows

he can throw whatever he wants to any batter at any time. His progress is very tangible, not only if you measure him statistically but if you scout him, too. He understands commanding the baseball, and he's got that great internal competitive mechanism."

Former All-Stars dotted the Angels outfield. With Bourjos running down everything in center, nine-time Gold Glove winner Torii Hunter moved to right, and three-time Gold Glove winner Vernon Wells took over in left as Bobby Abreu became the primary designated hitter. All three have multiple All-Star selections in their distinguished careers.

The infield has been manned by a quartet of versatile, athletic performers: Howie Kendrick, Erick Aybar, Maicer Izturis, and Alberto Callaspo. Kendrick is the primary second baseman, but can

Above Outfielder Mike Trout made his big league debut at the age of 19.

Below Vernon Wells, Peter Bourjos, and Torii Hunter gave the Angels one of baseball's best defensive outfielders.

"We all know what we need to do. I think we all play very similar styles, we have a lot of passion for it, and we have our priorities in line. I think that's only going to help us later on."

Above Mike Trout displays the skills that made him one of baseball's top prospects.

Above Right Alberto Callaspo makes another strong contribution to the Angels' attack.

Right Howie Kendrick developed into one of baseball's best defensive second basemen.

fill in at first and in left field. Aybar is the shortstop. Izturis plays second, third, and short, with Callaspo spending most of the time at third. Aybar, Izturis, and Callaspo are switch hitters, as is Conger, giving Scioscia more options when filling out a lineup card.

Further testimony to the development of the team was the selection of Weaver, Kendrick, and the rookie Walden to the 2011 All-Star team.

History and hope made the 2011 season a special one for the Angels and their legions of fans. Over five decades, the Angels organization has branded itself as one of the premier franchises in all of sports, annually being named one of the most fan-friendly teams in the country.

Led by the Angels Baseball Foundation, the team has become a pillar of the Southern California community. The foundation focuses on initiatives aimed to create and improve education, healthcare, arts and sciences, and community-related youth programs throughout the region, in addition to providing children the opportunity to experience the great game of baseball and its countless positive attributes.

The past has been filled with classic memories, but the future looks even more exciting, with an incomparable fan base and a committed ownership.

"We are fortunate to have an organization filled with individuals who understand the importance of community involvement," says Angels chairman Dennis Kuhl. "We thank Arte and his wife, Carole, for creating the Angels Baseball Foundation in 2004, which allows us to be involved in a variety of outreach programs.

"As an organization, we believe that it is not only a privilege to give back to the community that we live and work in, but it is also our responsibility. We have donated millions of dollars to life-changing causes, and we look forward to many more years of involvement in the greater Southern California market."

"Where the franchise is today is amazing," says longtime local TV personality Ed Arnold. "The dramatic rise in attendance is based on the fans' belief that ownership cares and is as passionate about winning as they are. It's just wonderful to go the stadium every night and see the sea of red.

"And the fact the team is so active in the community has further established their image as a positive and caring one."

Angel players, coaches, staff, and extended family all contribute to organizations in the greater Southern California market through numerous charitable donations and community appearances. The Angels host several events throughout the course of the season: the Children's Holiday Party, Little League Days, RBI Clinics, and Breaking Barriers, to

Below Garret Anderson returned to throw out a ceremonial first pitch.

Over five decades, the Angels organization has branded itself as one of the premier franchises in all of sports, annually being named one of the most fan-friendly teams in the country.

This Page Ervin Santana became the ninth pitcher in Angels history to toss a no-hitter, July 27, 2011 at Cleveland.

name a few. Some of the events involve partnerships with nonprofit groups including the Leukemia and Lymphoma Society, the Make-a-Wish Foundation, and the Second Harvest Food Bank. The organization has also implemented educational programs such as Rally Readers, Adopt-a-School, and Angels Scholars.

Included in this were funds from Major League Baseball's All-Star Legacy Grants, which were part of the Angels' hosting of the 2010 All-Star Game and its surrounding events. A significant portion of those funds were directed to the renovation of softball fields at Anaheim's Pioneer Park into the MLB Angels All-Star Complex. Two brand-new diamonds provide playing fields for underprivileged and special-needs youth in Orange County.

The Angels have touched more than 3,000 organizations, donating everything from funds to memorabilia, tickets, and ballpark experiences.

Among the Angels' notable beneficiaries are the Boys & Girls Clubs of Orange County, the Angels RBI Program, the Orangewood Children's Foundation, the Cystic Fibrosis Foundation, Special Olympics of Southern California, Healthy Smiles for Kids Orange County, the Children's Bureau of Orange County, the Anaheim Community Foundation, and the YMCA.

As the Angels celebrated their 50th anniversary season in 2011, they recalled many memorable moments, All-Star and Hall of Fame players, and, of course, a World Championship. And while the organization is proud of its many accomplishments on the field, perhaps an even greater satisfaction remains for the impact the team has had in its community efforts since the inception of the Angels.

The past has been filled with classic memories, but the future looks even more exciting, with an incomparable fan base and a committed ownership.

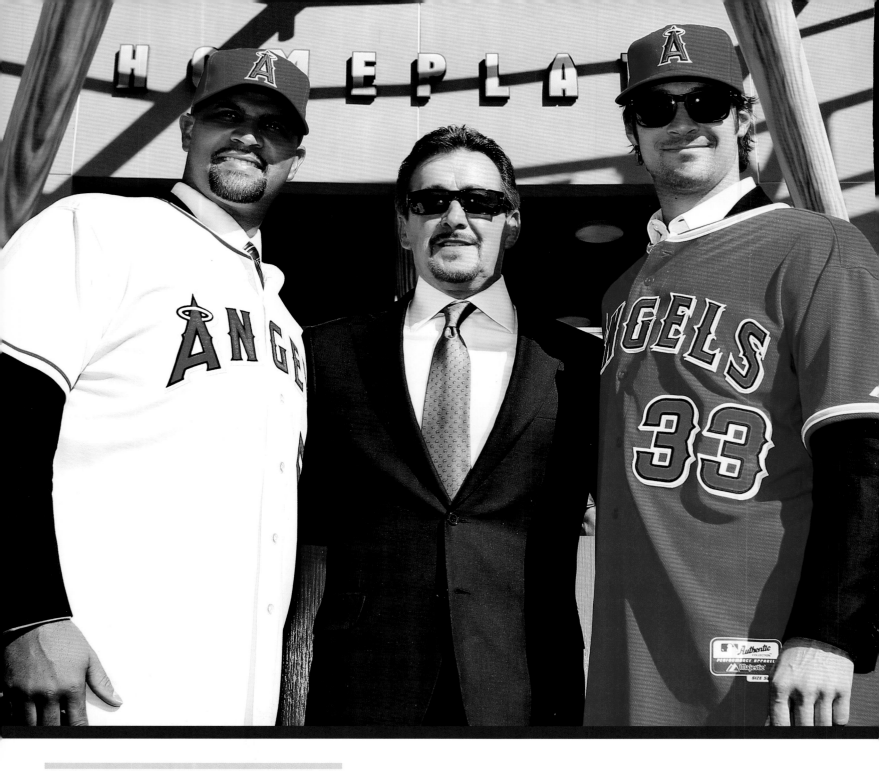

Above Angels owner Arte Moreno (center), flanked by free agent signees Albert Pujols (left) and C.J. Wilson (right).

THE NEXT FIFTY YEARS

After celebrating the Angels' 50th anniversary, owner Arte Moreno took bold steps to ensure the next fifty years will begin with a bang. In one dizzying day at major league baseball's Winter Meetings, Moreno signed slugger Albert Pujols and left-handed ace C.J. Wilson to ten-year and five-year contracts, respectively. The moves, which were celebrated during a surreal Angel Stadium press conference before over 4,000 adoring fans on December 10, 2011, established the Angels as a World Series favorite, transformed the Halos into a marquee team, and cemented the organization's reputation as a model franchise.

Top Manager Mike Scioscia and owner Arte Moreno listen as slugger Albert Pujols addresses Angel fans for the first time.

Bottom Arte Moreno welcomes Fountain Valley High School product C.J. Wilson back to Southern California by presenting him with an Angels cap and jersey.

Left When Albert Pujols—widely regarded as the best hitter of his generation—speaks, the baseball world listens.

Top Albert Pujols became intrigued with the Halos when Arte Moreno asked him to be part of the Angels family.

Opposite and Above Jerry Dipoto (opposite) joined manager Mike Scioscia (foreground) and president John Carpino (background) as part of the Angels brain trust on October 29; seven weeks later (above), he had orchestrated the additions of Albert Pujols, C.J. Wilson, Chris Iannetta, and LaTroy Hawkins.

COLOPHON

INSIGHT EDITIONS

Publisher: Raoul Goff

Executive Editor: Scott Gummer

Managing Editor: Kevin Toyama

Art Director: Jason Babler

Design Manager: Chrissy Kwasnik

Production Director: Anna Wan

Designers: MacFadden & Thorpe and Brad Mead

Photo Editor: Robert Binder

Copy Editor: Mikayla Butchart

Proofreader: Mark Nichol

INSIGHT EDITIONS would like to thank Bill Reuter, Amy Wideman, Jan Hughes, and Dagmar Trojanek.

ANGELS BASEBALL

Project Director: Tim Mead

Project Manager: Doug Ward

Project Coordinator: Jonathon Ciani

ANGELS BASEBALL would like to thank the following individuals and organizations who generously shared their rich collections to help make this book possible: Angels Baseball archives, Robert Binder, John Cordes, VJ Lovero, Debora Robinson, the Scott Garner Collection, the Tom Duino Collection, the *Orange County Register*, and the *Associated Press*.

The Angels would also like to thank the following staff members and contributors of AngelsWin.com for their contributions to this book: Chuck Richter, Geoff Bilau, Adam Dodge, David Saltzer, Victor Varadi, Bruce Nye, Sean Scanlon, Ricardo Ramos, Brent Hubbard, Lou Garcia, Kurt Swanson, Sean Dodds, Craig Malone, Thomas Crow, Geoff Stoddart, and Brian Ilten. Also, special thanks to Hall of Fame writer Ross Newhan for his valued contributions.